# Building Community

Christian

———

Caring

———

Vital

# Building Community

Christian

—

Caring

—

Vital

Loughlan Sofield

Rosine Hammett

Carroll Juliano

**AVE MARIA PRESS**   Notre Dame, Indiana 46556

International Standard Book Number: 0-87793-648-X

Cover and text design by Brian C. Conley.

Printed and bound in the United States of America.


*Library of Congress Cataloging-in-Publication Data*

Sofield, Loughlan.
    Building community : Christian, caring, vital / Loughlan Sofield,
Rosine Hammett, Carroll Juliano.
        p.    cm.
    Includes bibliographical references.
    ISBN  0-87793-648-X
    1. Community—Religious aspects—Catholic Church  2. Christian com-munities—Catholic Church  3. Catholic Church—Doctrines.    I. Hammett,
Rosine. II. Juliano, Carroll.    III. Title.
BX2347.7.S64              1998
262'.26—dc21                                                    97-35332
                                                                    CIP

*We dedicate this book with love to:*
*Barbara, Raymond, and Elizabeth,*
*Henry, S.J., and Bill, S.J.,*
*Rosie and Chester,*
*Don, Jonathan, Wyatt, Clayton,*
*and Victoria.*

# Acknowledgments

There are many individuals to whom we are indebted for their assistance in completing this book. We are grateful to Peter Holden, S.T., Julie McGuire, C.S.C., Malachy Sofield, S.T., and Bethania Whitehouse, C.S.C., for reading the manuscript and offering helpful recommendations. A very special thank-you is extended to Anne Bickford, S.H.C.J., who generously provided her expertise in the final editing of the manuscript.

We are deeply grateful to the computer "experts," Stephen Ernst, S.T., Julie McGuire, C.S.C., Paula Phillips, and Michael St. Pierre, who rescued us during some harrowing moments.

William Burkert, S.T., Jose Esquival, S.J., Sherry Immediato, and Paul Roy, S.T., allowed us the liberal use of material which they developed initially.

Frank Cunningham and Robert Hamma of Ave Maria Press, with their customary amiability, guided, encouraged, and supported us through every step of the process.

Finally, we express our thanks to our own communities which have sustained us in countless ways during the tedious moments of putting the finishing touches on this book.

# Contents

# *Foreword*

Shortly after ordination, I arrived at a parish where many shared my enthusiasm and eagerness to help bring small Christian communities to fruition. Rather quickly, I recognized the difficulties and frustrations that arise when the lofty ideals and theories associated with small communities encounter the realities of basic human interaction.

For example, one promising community within this parish had in it an individual who, consciously or otherwise, made rather grand gestures in the attempt to gain favor with perceived authority figures. Such displays sparked jealousy among the other members, which only hints at the interesting dynamics that gradually and progressively emerged within the group. Such a scenario served as a welcome to the real world of aspiring small communities.

The pastoral goal of "saving souls" has now long been questioned. There are no disembodied souls calling for pastoral attention floating around in our parishes. Rather, our communities consist of flesh and blood beings whose spiritual lives need to be nurtured within the human context. If we neglect such truths, our efforts will miss the mark.

Realizing and embracing our humanity allows for the introduction of small communities. Pietistic platitudes about small communities may stir interest and spur the initial steps, but in order to achieve long-run success, we must understand and deal with the totality of the persons who make up the community and, even more importantly, with the whole life and dynamic of the body of the community.

This is what is so remarkable about *Building Community— Christian, Caring, Vital*. It is real. It is human. The insights it offers into the human dynamics of small communities and the recommendations it proposes are invaluable, particularly in the areas of conflict, forgiveness, community decision-making, intimacy and confrontation.

The emphasis given to mission is especially gratifying. There is such hope for small Christian communities in our time. These hopes will surely be dashed if small communities are inwardly focused and remain in a comfort zone. The authors do well in forcing us to look carefully at processes for decision-making with regard to mission. Quite simply, "nice" people do not like to disagree or challenge one another. It is too easy to settle for the least common denominator in the community and, subsequently, lose our prophetic gift. Long-term evaluation of small Christian communities will look more to the fulfillment of Christ's mission than to whether communities limited themselves to a warm and satisfying experience.

Fortunately, the aforementioned group that faced the initial tension dealt with their issues and overcame their difficulties to flourish into a solid community. They collectively concentrated on the consciously shared commitment to social justice, outreach and mission, which strengthened their growth and development as a community. Similarly, *Building Community—Christian, Caring, Vital* serves as a clear and thoughtful compass to help navigate small communities from somewhat uncomfortable or even tumultuous origins to ultimately fulfilling destinations.

This book will be extremely helpful for parish communities, as well as for communities of women and men religious. The authors bring rich backgrounds of pastoral experience along with a love for people and an understanding of our human nature. Their personal insight into, as well as their thoughtful study of community enables them to share a wonderful gift with us all. We thank them for the deeply spiritual, practical ways they give us to enhance the development of those many small communities we value so much.

*—Thomas A. Kleissler*

# Introduction

Two realities confront society today: extreme individualism and the divorce of faith from ordinary family and social life. Yet in the midst of these seemingly negative factors, a quiet revolution is taking place in the hearts of many: a longing for community! Community and the hunger for community are not new phenomena. The concept of community is deeply embedded in the Christian tradition. This tradition acclaims God as the perfect community, a community of love. Life in community is the primary way in which God prepares us to participate in the divine life. The deeper we enter into community, the more we prepare ourselves for our relationship with God, both now and in the life to come.

In describing the way community facilitates our growth in the divine life, the National Conference of Catholic Bishops reminds us that community is the place where we grow in holiness, experience the healing power of Jesus, and are challenged to live our vocation as holy women and men. They further remind us that community is basic to our human nature.

> The challenge of being transformed into a holy person is not undertaken alone but within a faith community. . . . The longing for community touches each of us at the very core of our being. It is basic to being human, not "an extraneous addition, but a requirement" of our nature (*Catechism of the Catholic Church*, no. 1879). Within the community, we develop our potential, foster our talents, form our identity, and respond to the many challenges of being holy men and women. Community is not only an abstract principle but also a concrete reality lived each day at home, on campus, within society, and in organizations, movements and parishes. . . . Community is God's promise to those who have accepted the gracious invitation to live the Gospel and to be lights for the world.[1]

## Loneliness and the Need for Community

In contemporary society, the opportunity to participate in the divine life of community is severely curtailed. In a casual conversation, a friend likened our times to a rushing superhighway, a freeway with a stream of disconnected individuals, each plunging headlong on the highway toward some separate destination, in a car containing a single occupant, isolated and sealed in the machine. The drivers all move along at about the same speed, mesmerized by traffic and automatic in their responses. Each individual observes the other drivers with isolated indifference . . . the only communication through bumper stickers, e.g., "Have you hugged your child today?" The analogy is an appropriate description of the climate in today's society. The vacuum of interaction results in a society with a strong sense of loneliness, of isolation, of longing for relationships.

Sociologists have clearly identified this felt need for community in our current society. Wade Clark Roof has identified this need for belonging as primary among the "baby boomers," those he aptly describes as the "generation of seekers."[2] The longing for community, however, is not restricted to this age group. It has also been confirmed by the recent research of George Gallup of the Princeton Research Center.[3] Gallup identifies a sense of community as one of the greatest needs of contemporary Americans. The study reports that three out of every ten Americans are experiencing great loneliness. We suspect that similar research conducted in other developed countries would produce corresponding results.

In an article about the United States Bill of Rights, Australian Jesuit Frank Brennan has insightfully identified one contributing factor to this phenomenon within American culture.[4] His visit to the United States was prompted by an interest in studying the Bill of Rights. His stated goal was to determine whether such a document should be drafted for Australia. Brennan's conclusion could be summarized as: "Keep it. We don't want it." He believes that our interpretation of the Bill of Rights has created a society so concerned with individual rights that the common good suffers. We might ask: Have we idealized personalism to the point that the communal good remains only as a nostalgic reminder of a long-forgotten past? Is this individualism endemic to our society, or can this lost spirit of community be revived? How can we begin to form stronger communities of growth, of faith? What is necessary for a group to become a truly apostolic faith community? These questions, combined with our beliefs in the value of community, provided the motivation to develop this book.

## What Is Community?

The term "community" as we use it in this book is intended to be a far-reaching and inclusive concept. It encompasses a variety of forms of community: prayer groups, support groups, Renew groups, small faith communities, church organizations, religious congregations, any gathering of committed Christians. Although we have focused our attention on relatively small interpersonal communities, much of the material presented can also be applied to entire parishes. Our experience in working with parishes verifies this application.

A Christian community is a small group of persons who come together on a regular basis to foster their spiritual, personal, and/or apostolic growth. The forms it takes are varied. Some groups gather to pray, to read scripture, and to build bonds of love, forgiveness, and unity. Some focus on sharing their faith stories and life experiences. Others have an explicit apostolic mission.

Still others, like religious congregations, gather like-minded and committed people into vowed communities. Though the forms are many, the living of the gospel is at the heart of each of these communities. Dynamic Christian communities are most often characterized by a climate in which members feel free to share honestly about their joys and sorrows, their successes and failures, and their sickness and struggle in the midst of the realities of their daily lives.

This kind of relationship in community does not occur instantly or easily. It evolves in an organic way. It requires that people remain in the community long enough to establish a relationship that supports working through the inevitable group dynamics and acting in a unified manner.

Our experience over the years with many types of communities in many countries and cultures has convinced us that there are certain dynamics which operate when persons come together, regardless of culture or country. This book is designed to assist the reader in understanding some of these dynamics and exploring ways which will contribute to the growth of the community.

## Common Obstacles to Community

Assumptions about community, especially those assumptions that are never given voice, serve as major obstacles to the development of healthy, vibrant, life-giving communities.

One such assumption is that Christian groups, e.g., prayer groups, are exempt from the ordinary dynamics which occur in other groups. The myth is that these communities will not experience the same dynamics found in other groups because they are engaged in a "holy" endeavor. Perhaps this myth originates in the over-idealized perception of the early Christian community, the "perfect" community, described in the second and fourth chapters of the Acts of the Apostles. No mention is made in these two chapters of the ordinary human dynamics that occurred. However, careful reading of the remaining chapters describing the early Christian community reveals a group that encountered all the normal dynamics present in groups. Since the early church communities were composed of persons like ourselves, these communities experienced all the dynamics we find in present day communities.

Don Brophy, the managing editor of Paulist Press, in an article he authored, indicated that one of the main reasons many prayer groups and communities established in the early post-Vatican II period disintegrated was the lack of awareness and understanding of the dynamics encountered when the groups came together as community.[5]

In any group there are forces operating at an unconscious level. This is a perfectly normal phenomenon. These forces arise from the inner relationships among group members as well as from external forces. Human emotions, feelings, needs, personalities, and relationships form the interpersonal network of group life. These dynamics can be managed in ways that lead to productive group

15

outcomes that leave members with positive attitudes toward groups. For this to occur, the dynamics must be recognized. If the dynamics within a group are not recognized and understood, problems will arise that have the potential to destroy the group.

# The Purpose of This Book

There is a plethora of books on the market today that focus on the theological and spiritual dimensions of community. In addition, there are a number of content-oriented books that provide scripture-based materials on community sharing. What influenced our decision to write this book was the scarcity of texts that explain the normal dynamics of communities, such as trust, anger, forgiveness, and reconciliation, as well as the skills of listening, conflict resolution, and confrontation.

Knowledge of these issues, combined with a general understanding of group process, can assist group members to participate in community more constructively. For instance, they can be better prepared to:

- see the relationship between what is spoken and its effect on both speaker and listener;
- respond appropriately to each other's feelings, ideas, and perceptions;
- incorporate members who feel excluded;
- handle individual and community problems;
- create the conditions that facilitate learning.

We also heard from communities that had used our previous text asking for some definite processes for building community. There seemed to be a need and desire for a "workbook." Therefore, we have attempted to construct such a practical book to be used by both new and existing communities. While not every chapter will be relevant to each community, we would recommend that every community utilize the suggested processes in Section I.

Section I consists of three chapters. Chapter 1 describes the developmental stages of community. Chapter 2 provides a model for understanding the interdynamics that occur in communities. Chapter 3 explores the beliefs about community that directly affect the development of community.

Section II consists of a number of chapters that can be used as discussion material for communities. The chapters in this section deal with specific elements of group development, e.g., the importance of listening, dealing with conflict and confrontation, understanding the role of anger and forgiveness, building trust, the effects of transition and termination, and a variety of other issues and dynamics that affect every community.

Included in every chapter are questions for reflection, supplementary readings on the subject, and a suggested process to facilitate discussion and growth. The processes are only suggestions. Each group can evaluate the process and discern which approach will best meet its specific needs.

We have used a number of examples throughout the text. While the examples may have occurred in a specific type of community, we have selected only those examples which we feel are universal and have relevance for any community.

When a reference is made to a work listed in the suggested readings found at the end of each chapter, we have not footnoted that reference. Other references not included in the suggested reading are footnoted.

## Conclusion

God calls us to community. Through community we can be helped to discover our truest and deepest selves. Relationships in community help us to discover the fullness of who we are. As Paul says in his letter to the Corinthians, "You are all one body, members of one another."

The outpouring of the Spirit at Pentecost was not to isolated persons, but was a gift to the gathered community. The Spirit was given to the Body of Christ—the community.

# Section I

# *Dynamics of Community*

# *1*
# *Stages of Group Development*

Have you even been part of a community that was fun, recreative, and energizing? Can you identify a community experience that was draining, de-energizing, and stagnant? You can probably answer "yes" to both questions.

Every community experience has the potential to be life-giving or life-draining. The outcome depends on how well the members understand the very normal group dynamics that occur in any community.

Angelo D'Agostino, a Jesuit-psychiatrist, declared in a conversation with the authors that in the post-Vatican II church people are healed and saved in the context of community. Given this belief, he advises that since a community is a group, anyone wishing to be effective in building community must be trained and knowledgeable about the dynamics that occur in all groups.

The material in this section sets a context for the chapters that follow. It provides a brief understanding of the dynamics that affect communities. This knowledge can assist in the development of more life-giving communities.

## Basic Group Theory

There are two basic approaches to groups. One approach is to focus on the individuals in the group. Those trained and formed to be sensitive to the needs of the individual, such as pastoral ministers, spiritual directors, or counselors, often opt for this approach.

The second approach is to focus on the group as a whole. This approach assumes that the group is more than the sum of its parts: the group has a life and dynamics of its own. There are constant, unconscious dynamics occurring within the group. Attending to group rather than individual dynamics will help clarify what is transpiring on an unconscious level within the group. Gaining this knowledge increases the likelihood for both personal and communal growth. While the major focus is on the group dynamic, i.e., what is occurring within the group's life, this approach need not ignore the individuals who comprise the group.

We believe that the first approach, the focus on the individual in the group, is often what prevents community growth. While this approach may aid the individual in personal understanding and growth, it fails to encompass the powerful dynamics that are supra-personal and that profoundly affect every member. Effective community leaders continue to increase their knowledge of the group as a whole and to employ the skills of group dynamics in order to further the movement of the group toward growth. With this knowledge and these skills as their backdrop, leaders can perceive individual comments and behaviors in an unconventional way. They realize that an individual's actions may convey the unconscious beliefs of the entire group. The reactions of group members to the individual's behavior, supportive or passive, unknowingly speaks volumes about the group's convictions. Failure to comprehend this phenomenon often condemns a group to understanding only the most superficial aspects of the group's life.

Learning to think of the group as a whole does not come easily to most people. It demands training and supervision to overcome the natural reaction which focuses only on the seemingly logical behavior of individuals.

## Community Stages

There are many group dynamics that affect the development of community. We addressed many of these dynamics in an earlier work.[1] It is helpful to revisit and develop one chapter of that book which can serve as a primer for the chapters to follow. These dynamics are described in "Stages in the Development of Community." The proposed model emerges from decades of experience of working with communities.

Most people are familiar with the theory of stages as it applies to individuals: each person grows and develops through somewhat predictable stages, beginning with earliest childhood and proceeding through a number of stages into late adulthood. Erik Erikson describes these stages as epigenetic, i.e., building one upon the other.[2] The dynamic of stages is observable in communities as well, proceeding through some fairly predictable patterns and usually in a developmental and sequential fashion. To the degree that leaders understand these stages, they will be in a position to foster the healthier development of the community. Stages are artificial, but they provide a paradigm for understanding the inner workings of community. While different members of the community can be experiencing different stages, at a given time there is usually a predominate, discernible stage that characterizes the group as a whole.

Table 1.1, which follows, is an outline of this section. We suggest that you use the material presented in this section to evaluate your own community, by asking a series of questions:

- At which stage do we see ourselves?
- What is the task we must address at this stage to continue our communal growth?
- What obstacles make it difficult for us to grow through this stage?

Table 1.1
# Stages in the Development of a Community

| Stage | Expressed Feeling or Behavior | Predominant Need | Function of Leader | Tasks of Leader |
|---|---|---|---|---|
| 1. Orientation | Anxiety, fear or insecurity | Safety and security | Create a climate where people feel safe and secure | Clarify expectations |
| 2. In/Out | Fight, flight or neurotic behavior | Belonging | Help those alienated to experience a sense of belonging | Encourage those who feel alienated discuss their perceptions |
| 3. Up/Down | Competitiveness | Esteem | Initiate a process that fosters personal value esteem | Utilize a gift discernment process |
| 4. Conflict | Avoidance and denial | Safety and esteem | Encourage the community to deal with the conflict | Model a willingness to deal with conflict |
| 5. Cohesion | Peace and trust, tendency to nest | Belonging | Call the group to its mission | Challenge the community to focus beyond itself |
| 6. Faith-Sharing | Ambivalence | Safety and esteem | Invite the community to engage in faith-sharing | Model faith-sharing |
| 7. Near/Far | Struggle to find a comfort level | Love or affinity | Aid the community to clarify expectations of intimacy | Invite members to discuss expectations of intimacy |
| 8. Termination | Sadness and anger | Safety | Help community process the experience of loss | Assist the community with the process of grieving |

# First Stage—Orientation

The orientation stage is the initial stage in the life of every community. This stage occurs not only when a group begins, but also when there is a change of membership within the group. When a community adds a new member or loses a current member, it becomes, in essence and reality, a new community. For continued growth to occur, the community must focus again on the tasks germane to the stage of orientation.

When working with new communities we request that the group identify and articulate their feelings during this initial phase. Responders consistently reflect feelings of anxiety, fear, or insecurity, coupled with the sense of excitement and hope at the new beginning. But it is the feelings of insecurity, fear, and anxiety that have the most powerful, and potentially detrimental, influence on members during this early stage.

We then ask new members to describe the observable behavior connected with these emotions. This request produces a long list of somewhat predictable behaviors, including withdrawal, silence, boisterousness, aggressiveness, hostility, shows of bravado, etc.

The key to understanding the dynamic of the orientation stage lies in helping individuals to realize that behavior is normally an indication of a human need. Most human behavior is need-directed. For example, in an attempt to meet the human need of belonging, a person may become overly compliant in a group, agreeing with everything that is said, even agreeing to contradicting statements. Unknowingly, people may react to the behavior without attempting to understand its cause, or the specific need behind it.

During the orientation stage when feelings of fear, anxiety, and uncertainty are predominant, the group's primary need is for safety and security. Observable behavior is simply a means of compensating for and detaching from these unpleasant feelings.

The role of the leader at this stage is to create a climate in which the members can feel safe and secure. There are a number of ways to achieve this. The most successful way is to clarify expectations with questions such as:

- What do the members expect of the leader?
- What does the leader expect of the members?
- What do the members expect of each other?
- What are the acceptable or unacceptable norms and behavior for the group?
- What are the common, agreed upon expectations regarding confidentiality determining what will and will not be shared outside the group?

In the previous paragraph we highlighted the leader's responsibility for creating a climate of safety and security. It is our conviction that every member of the group also bears responsibility for sharing that role of leadership. Therefore, when the term "leader" appears in this book, we ask you to extend it to include all members of the group. No one person should be burdened with complete responsibility for the life of the group. Communities that expect a single person to bear full responsibility for the success of the group evolve into passive, dependent communities. This statement does not negate the role of leadership in communities. Quite the contrary. Leadership is one of the charisms mentioned by Saint Paul in his letter to the Romans (12:6-8). In our experience, leaderless groups and communities are ineffective. We believe that groups and communities require designated leadership if they are to be effective. The presence of leadership does not absolve the group from assuming responsibility for its growth and development. The more responsibility members assume, the more they empower themselves.

## Stage One Summary

During the orientation stage members feel anxious and fearful, and these feelings are expressed in a variety of behaviors. At this stage it is important to respond to the need and not react to the behavior. Only when individuals feel safe and secure will they proceed to the next stage. In the orientation stage communities struggle with the issue of trust (see also chapter 4).

## Reflection Questions

1. How do we orient new members?
2. What do we do to create a climate of safety and security?
3. What unresolved mistrust from the past is affecting our building community today?

## Second Stage—In/Out

A feeling or sense of belonging characterizes the second stage. Some members feel a part of the group; they have a sense of belonging. In contrast to those who feel "in," others feel "out"—outside of the group. They experience a sense of alienation. This basic need to belong, to experience a connection with others, is the primary reason that some people join communities.

It is important to note that progression through these stages is developmental and is usually unconscious. The fact that those belonging to the "in" group are insensitive to other members' feeling excluded is not a condemnation of them. The members who feel "in" the group presume that, because they experience a sense of belonging, everyone feels that same sense of inclusion.

The need to feel a sense of belonging is a powerful drive. When this basic need is frustrated, the normal reactions are fight or flight. Reactions may be pronounced when excluded from a community where one has a strong need or desire for acceptance.

Some members who experience alienation develop very aggressive responses and appear to be in constant battle with the

25

community, disputing every suggestion, recommendation, and tradition. Others assume a flight mode, which usually results in either termination of membership or in minimal involvement by living on the periphery of the group. Anna Freud offers a third possible reaction for those who feel as though they don't belong. She claims that, when the basic need for belonging is not met, persons often become neurotic. The observation of strange and neurotic behavior among members of the community can invite the community to examine whether they have truly integrated the fringe members. Too often the community merely condemns the behavior.

While a sense of alienation and the resulting behavior occurs in communities, it is important to realize this same dynamic also occurs in the larger society. Those who do not experience a sense of belonging often revert to fight, flight, or neurotic behavior.

In each group there are different criteria for determining those who feel "in"—who belong—and those who feel "out"—who feel excluded. The status of "in" or "out" can be determined by such things as length of time in the community, age, sex, culture, and personal influence on the group. The best way to discover whether or not the group is at this stage is to inquire directly whether there are members who feel as though they are not accepted and don't belong. Unless the question is raised directly, those in the "in" group remain convinced that everyone feels a sense of belonging. Recently we worked with a parish community who prided themselves on their ability to fully integrate all members. We inquired if some members felt alienated or unaccepted. Our question was met with a resounding, "No. Everyone in this parish feels completely welcome." When we questioned further whether anyone felt differently, one courageous woman spoke of the alienation she had felt since becoming a member of the community. She had never voiced her frustration. Only the direct question elicited her response.

There are individuals who choose to remain on the periphery of the community. Every attempt to include them is met with resistance. These are individuals who often find satisfaction in being in the role of the alienated and rejected victim. In some perverse way it provides them with a sense of power and self-righteousness. Their position on the fringe meets some personal need. At some point a community must accept that they have done everything possible to incorporate these individuals and cease attempting to incorporate them. Not every person has the capacity to be incorporated into every community (see chapter 5).

## Stage Two Summary

The second stage in the life of a community is the in/out stage. Here the basic need is to belong. The task of leadership (members) is to probe the resistance and invite those who feel a sense of alienation to verbalize this feeling. The "in" group will usually have difficulty realizing that anyone is experiencing alienation.

## Reflection Questions

1. Who are the members who feel alienated?
2. How do we include and integrate everyone in the community?
3. What are our criteria for establishing who is "in" and who is "out"?

## Third Stage—Up/Down

It is difficult at times to ascertain whether the group is in stage two or stage three. People are unsure whether they feel alienated, devalued, or both. There is often a perceptible overlap between these two stages.

In the third stage the predominant need is for esteem, both self-esteem and the esteem of others. It is a normal dynamic for a community, usually in an unconscious way, to stratify members along a continuum ranging from the most to the least important, valued, and esteemed. Those, of course, who see themselves as least important feel devalued and react accordingly.

The ways in which this differentiation is made will be different for each group. Some of the criteria by which status is judged are income, longevity within the community, speaking ability, social status, perceived power, education, roles, and relationship to authority figures.

It is relatively easy to discern when a group is at this third stage because the predominant spirit is one of competition. Competitive behavior is evident at this time because it is the vehicle for individuals to satisfy their need for esteem. Therefore, conversations within the community center around personal accomplishments and status.

At this stage the primary task is to help each member recognize his or her personal value to the community. There are many ways to accomplish this. The most effective way we have discovered is to utilize a group discernment process (see chapter 6). Such a process encourages the group to value the unique gifts that each member brings to the community. Discerning the gifts of each member helps to heighten the esteem and minimize the competitive climate.

## Stage Three Summary

During the third stage the members have a strong desire to feel valued. This stage is characterized by a competitive spirit. Any process that accents the value of each person and his or her contribution to the community is appropriate at this stage.

*discernment*

## Fourth Stage—Conflict

Regardless of all the positive steps taken by the community, the group will still experience conflict. Conflict is an inevitable stage in the life of every community, and faith communities are no exception. Actually, conflict has been an inherent part of the Christian community. The New Testament is replete with accounts of conflict within the early church: the apostles arguing over who is most important (Lk 9); Paul and Barnabas engaging in a "sharp disagreement" over whether to take Mark as a companion on their apostolic journey (Acts 15); the "controversy" regarding circumcision at the Council of Jerusalem (Acts 15).

Conflict is, without doubt, the most difficult stage for most Christian communities. There is a prevailing myth that a good Christian community should be immune to conflict. The *Notre Dame Study of Catholic Parish Life* puts this myth to rest when it states that, "The absence of conflict in a parish (or in any Christian community) is more likely a sign of *rigor mortis* than of vitality and community."[3]

It is evident from Table 1.1 (page 23) that a community does not begin to develop a sense of cohesion, become comfortable enough to share faith, or create an environment which encourages intimacy until it has successfully traversed the stage of conflict by either managing or resolving the conflict.

Conflict is normally painful, and most healthy people will make every effort to avoid pain. However, there can no true community until the group is willing to confront and address it. The issue of conflict is developed in chapter 7. The Christian response to conflict is forgiveness, which is addressed in chapter 8.

In order to build effective, life-giving communities there must be a willingness to embrace conflict. This choice demands a concrete act of the will, since the natural inclination is to avoid it. After the conflict, substantial energy must be directed toward fostering the process of forgiveness.

## Stage Four Summary

Avoidance is the normal reaction to conflict. Management or resolution of conflict is essential if continued growth is to occur. However, unless the members are willing to work at managing or resolving the conflict, the community will never become a life-giving community. The task of leadership is to encourage the members to address the conflict.

# Fifth Stage—Cohesion

A community achieves a spirit of unity, peace, and cohesion only after it has engaged in conflict. Avoidance of conflict prevents the ultimate growth of the community. It is the very struggle with conflict that creates the condition where the community begins to sense a togetherness, a cohesion.

The stage of cohesion is a very productive time in the life of the community. The climate of trust allows community members to engage in common endeavors and to take greater risks with each other.

Coupled with these positive results are two areas of concern that can also arise within the community during this time. The  first concern during this cohesiveness is a tendency to "nest." The community can become self-absorbed, focusing more on self-maintenance than on the call to mission. We begin from the assumption that Christian community always has an external mission as one of its goals (see chapter 9). At this point the role of the leader is to challenge the members to maintain a balance between a community that supports members and a community that focuses on mission.

The second concern is a dynamic called "group think" that can emerge during this cohesive stage and can become an obstacle to growth. "Group think" can take a number of forms. One of the more prevalent forms is decision-making based more on the preservation of the peace and harmony of the community than on responding to gospel imperatives. We have seen this dynamic develop in previously productive communities with disastrous results. Groups that have a clear apostolic mission opt for the comfort of a nesting, "teddy-bear" community over the demands of the mission. The responsibility of leadership is to challenge the group to go beyond the comfort and security of cohesion to the less comfortable call to Christian ministry and service.

Given the dynamic of "group think," the cohesive stage is the least effective time to use consensus as the primary vehicle for decision-making. Too frequently the group develops unspoken and unconscious criteria for decision-making based on maintaining the peace and unity of the community. Peace and unity take precedence over mission. Chapter 10 develops our understanding and concerns about communities that opt for consensus as the only form of decision-making.

## Stage Five Summary

The cohesive stage is a comfortable stage, characterized by peace, unity, and trust. The continued growth and life of the community can be threatened at this stage by the temptation to "nest."

## Reflection Questions

1. When have I observed a tendency to "nest"?
2. Are we opting for security rather than the uncomfortableness of challenge?
3. Does mission continue to be our motivating force?

## Sixth Stage—Faith-Sharing

One of the major factors that distinguishes a Christian faith community from other communities is the sharing of faith. Many people enter Christian community with the explicit intent to share faith. Some communities even have this as their primary purpose.

Faith-sharing demands a climate of trust. The members have to believe they can trust others with the most personal, intimate, and sacred part of themselves, their faith life and experiences.

Faith-sharing that occurs prior to the time when there is a climate of trust, safety, and security is usually somewhat superficial. After the community has dealt successfully with conflict and achieved a sense of relative cohesion, there is both a desire and a readiness to share faith. This desire is mixed with a fear of sharing this most intimate part of oneself with others. Desire coupled with fear create the general ambivalence characteristic of this stage.

Two things are necessary for the successful movement through this stage: sufficient trust to allow people to risk the sharing of their faith journey and the leaders' willingness to model for the group by sharing their own faith story.

Communities living together, such as religious congregations, are usually hesitant about sharing faith. When the suggestion is made to share faith, it is often met with intense resistance. Probably numerous reasons exist for this reaction. Three obvious reasons are: a lack of trust, a fear of being perceived as hypocritical by those with whom one lives, and a concern that the poverty of one's faith life will be revealed. The more perfectionism is a part of the personal or congregational history, the greater the degree of difficulty for members to share faith. Chapter 11 is devoted to this issue of faith-sharing in greater detail.

## Stage Six Summary

Christian communities should be faith-sharing communities. However, there is a general ambivalence about sharing faith. The task of leadership is to create a climate where the members feel comfortable sharing this personal, intimate part of themselves.

## Reflection Questions
1. When do we truly share faith?
2. What fears prevent me entering into faith-sharing?
3. How has sharing faith affected us as a community?

## Seventh Stage—Near/Far

Every community ultimately must deal with the question, "How close and intimate do I really want to become with these people?" The near/far stage is the stage when the community struggles with the issue of intimacy. Given the fact that many people enter communities to achieve intimacy, it may be a disappointment to find that intimacy in community is not achieved until many previous stages have been successfully navigated.

A community at this stage is like a carefully orchestrated dance. A patterned sequence of approach and withdrawal can be observed. Members are in search of a level of intimacy and sharing where they can feel comfortable. This dance is influenced by two key issues: (1) discovering a balance among the varying intimacy needs of the different members; and (2) whether or not the individual members have developed some capacity for personal intimacy outside the parameters of the community.

Usually, the more people have developed intimate relationships outside the community, the less need they have for strong bonds of intimacy among community members and the greater their capacity to contribute at this stage. The attempt to find a comfortable communal level is fraught with tension. The needs and expectations of the members can run a wide gamut from wanting constant intimacy to not wanting any intimacy within the community. It becomes a real challenge to locate that satisfactory point where the members can, as one person has said, "find space in their togetherness."

The second key issue is one that is often overlooked in evaluating communities, i.e., whether the members have acquired a level of individual maturity sufficient for establishing intimate relationships. There may be members who, while desiring a high level of intimacy in community, experience constant frustration. They are expecting community to meet intimacy needs that must first be met at a personal level.

Often, too, there is a reluctance in members at this stage to expend the energy required to build intimacy within the community because they are aware that termination is imminent. They engage in a mental dialogue that says, "Why bother getting close when soon we are going to say good-bye?" Aware of this tendency, leadership's role is to challenge the community to deal with the process of termination.

In a later chapter the issue of intimacy will be explored further (see chapter 12).

## Stage Seven Summary

Individuals bring different needs and expectations for intimacy into community. Given this spectrum, the task is to establish a level acceptable to all members. Developing one's personal capacity for intimacy is a foundation for attaining intimacy in community.

## Reflection Questions

1. What level of intimacy do I expect and desire in community?
2. When do we discuss our expectations regarding intimacy?
3. What fosters intimacy in this community?

## Eighth Stage—Termination

While conflict is typically the most difficult stage, termination is the second most difficult. Termination, as we will be using the term, covers a wide range of experiences that are associated with endings, e.g., separation, transition, loss, and actual termination. Communities do not live in perpetuum; they exist for a limited time. Once membership changes, the community as it existed ceases and a new community comes into existence. Failure to accept this reality is a stumbling block to continued growth. The basic conviction regarding loss is, "You can't say hello until you've learned to say good-bye." Communities that avoid the reality of endings condemn themselves to stagnation. Unless a community proceeds through the process of termination (see chapter 13), it will not allow new life to be generated within the community. Communities that avoid termination generally resist the inclusion of new members.

Traditionally, we are a church that is rich in ritual for celebrating endings and loss. Yet what is missing from our tradition is a process of intentional grieving to accompany the celebration. Loss is an extremely painful experience, and the normal reaction is an avoidance of emotions that are evoked. An unconscious collusion to avoid the process of dealing with termination can dominate the community. All members, including the designated leaders, can be lured into the resistance. Unless leadership disengages from the resistance, there is increased possibility that the generative life of the community will be diminished. This stage, along with the stage of conflict, may be the one where outside resources are most needed.

In conducting workshops on community stages we have invited the community to deal first with the stage of termination before discussing the stage of orientation. The community frequently discovers that following this approach and focusing on termination initially frees them to look more realistically at the process of orientation.

## Stage Eight Summary

Termination is a difficult but essential stage in the life of every community. Failure to address this dynamic sabotages future community building. There is an unconscious collusion to avoid the painful experience of endings.

## Reflection Questions

1. What previous losses in my life are unfinished business?
2. How does our community address loss?
3. How can we deal with termination more effectively in the future?

## Suggested Reading

Baranowski, Arthur R. *Creating Small Faith Communities*. Cincinnati, OH: St. Anthony Messenger Press, 1988.

## Process for Group Sharing

The following process is designed to encourage the participants to apply the theory of stages of community development to the present community. Use the information you have generated at the end of each stage to help you respond to the following questions.

- At which stage do we see ourselves?
- What is the task we must address at this stage to continue our communal growth?
- What obstacles make it difficult for us to grow through this stage?

Invite each person who wishes to share his or her responses to these questions. Then the group can engage in general dialogue. At the end of the discussion pose one final question: "Based on our perceptions, what do we need to do in this community to foster further growth?"

# 2
# A Model for Understanding Community Interactions

In addition to the group dynamic discussed in the previous chapter, the other important dynamic at work in a community is the interpersonal dynamics between and among members. These dynamics have an effect on the community. This chapter summarizes a model of interdynamics developed by Stephen Ober and David Kantor. Their model assesses team functioning and has relevance for community.

There are numerous models and paradigms that enhance both personal growth and group interactions. They can be valuable tools in fostering growth in self-understanding and self-change. Regrettably, some individuals use such paradigms to analyze the other members. The principal goal of studying such models is to better understand one's own behavior and to discern ways to change. Edwin Friedman, a systems analyst, proposes that if you want to change and motivate others, you need to focus on self-definition, i.e., changing yourself.[1]

The model has a value for community as well because reflecting on it can lead to new insights on dysfunctional dynamics that impede the growth of community. These insights increase the possibility for promoting constructive change.

## Basic Types of Behavior

The Kantor Four-Player System model proposes four types of behavior or roles that people characteristically assume in groups. These roles affect the development and performance of the group/community:

**Basic Behaviors**

1. A **move** initiates a sequence of behavior.
2. A **follow** supports a move.
3. An **oppose** opposes a move.
4. A **bystand** observes and makes comments that move the group along.

35

For example, in a community, member "A" proposes that the group should terminate its existence because it has become stagnant (a move). Member "B" responds by indicating agreement with what "A" has proposed (a follow). Member "C" indicates a strong disagreement with what has been proposed (an oppose). After a slight pause member "D" suggests that the group has become rather moribund, but also indicates that it still has the potential to be effective, if the group is willing to take certain, defined steps to rectify the situation (a bystand).

Each of these four behaviors is necessary for the effective functioning of the team/group/community. The challenge is to assure that all four behaviors are operative in the normal functioning of community. The most effective communities are those in which there is a balance among all these functions and where individual members are encouraged to develop their capacity to perform a number of functions rather than become fixated on only one behavior.

## Potential Obstacles

There are potential obstacles in the model that could impede the effective functioning of the community. One is that the community values only one or two selective behaviors, and this would result in utilizing only one or two of the functions.

A second potential obstacle is discouragement or deprecation of those behaviors that are considered inappropriate, ineffective, or non-valued by community members.

All four behaviors are required for maximum effectiveness of the community because each performs a different but necessary function. The absence of any one of these functions would seriously impair the growth of the community.

### The Function of Each Behavior

A **move** provides direction.
A **follow** enables completion.
An **oppose** creates correction.
A **bystand** offers perspective.

A move is an initiating action. It is performed by the person who takes the initiative to suggest an action or direction for the community. No suggestion moves a community to action unless there are people who agree with the suggestion and support it, i.e., followers. Often the suggested action appears in its "raw" form, proposed by a single individual who has either not wanted to nor been capable of seeing some of the pitfalls present. Hence, there is a need for an opposer. This is the individual or individuals who provide the reality check by questioning or challenging the proposal. The final function is provided by the bystanders, who provide the objective insight on the dynamics that are occurring and on the positive or negative effect on the development of the community.

36

# Behavioral Archetypes

Ober and Kantor identify many dynamics which occur frequently and which can be detrimental to the functioning, effectiveness, and growth of the community. These dynamics, called "behavioral archetypes," can be found in most communities. Understanding the dynamic is the first step in rectifying dysfunctional behavior. The three behavioral archetypes that follow are, in our opinion, the most common in Christian communities.

## Point-Counterpoint

The first of these archetypes is point-counterpoint, characterized by two behaviors: move-oppose. This archetype is described by other theorists as negative pairing. In point-counterpoint one person initiates by making a suggestion, thereby providing a sense of direction. This action is immediately met by a counterpoint, i.e., the stating of an opposing position. This dynamic is operative in a community when a few members are engaged in the discussion and a significant number take a passive-observer role. Their passiveness subtly encourages the ever-expanding move-oppose dynamic. This is a dynamic that you have probably witnessed countless times. It is reminiscent of a tennis match where the opposing players drive the ball farther and farther into the opponent's court in a seemingly endless volley. Although fully emotionally engaged in the "match," the audience silently observes the athletic battle from a physically detached position.

The point-counterpoint archetype is most frequently found in situations and cultures that are highly competitive, where the norm is one of win/lose. This behavior usually results from a leadership style that tends to pit people against each other.

There are leadership responses that will help move the group beyond this behavior. Leaders (and, as stated in chapter 1, every member has a responsibility for leadership) have to act in an assertive manner. The first step is to point out the negative effect the behavior has on the functioning of the community. Next, invite and encourage members to assume the role of bystanders by helping to bring light and wisdom to a discussion that is producing only heat and polarization. When the win/lose atmosphere is relatively pervasive, leaders can affirm and reward the behavior that is more collaborative. The role of leadership is to develop structures and create a climate within the community that both fosters openness and encourages disagreement without fear of reprisal or punishment.

## Courteous Compliance

The second archetype is identified as courteous compliance, characterized by a move-follow sequence. Others theorists have described this behavior as "group think." Courteous compliance is characterized by an unwillingness to disagree with the leader.

The followers indiscriminately and blindly follow whatever the leader proposes. Critics of "group think" offer the Bay of Pigs fiasco as a prime example. Although the cabinet members and advisors who met with President Kennedy knew that the endeavor was doomed to failure, no one was willing to disagree with the president. They blindly followed and enthusiastically affirmed whatever he proposed.

While point-counterpoint is generally found in highly competitive cultures, courteous compliance will most likely exist in a traditional, hierarchical culture, especially one that tends to avoid confrontation with designated leaders. The tendency to avoid not only confrontation, but also conflict, controversy, and the acknowledgment of any negative issues, results in a community that is bland, generic, and almost never prophetic.

A notable characteristic of courteous compliance is the reaction toward any member who attempts to threaten this seemingly peaceful climate. There is a powerful commitment to group loyalty. Anyone who appears to be disloyal or who challenges the status quo is ostracized. This attitude of uncompromising loyalty is especially directed toward designated leaders. The members clearly communicate that questioning the leader's decisions will be considered anathema. This lack of critical judgment results in a community that appears to foster a strong sense of unity and solidarity, but lacks any unified commitment to the leader's decisions.

The most useful and fruitful intervention to employ in countering courteous compliance is to encourage "loyal" opposition (i.e., supporting opposition and bystander functions) and to offer creative alternatives. An effective way to accomplish this is by raising questions and engaging the members in the search for solutions. This challenges members to clarify and re-evaluate their positions.

With each of these archetypical behaviors it is helpful to provide interventions that aid members in understanding the negative effect their behavior has on community.

## Covert Opposition

The third of these archetypal behaviors is covert opposition in which the normal behavioral sequence is move-follow or move-bystand. This has been described in other models as passive-aggressive behavior. In this sequence the initial movement is met by apparent agreement, but, in actuality, this response is one of indirect or passive resistance and sabotaging. This covert opposition or passive-aggressive behavior is generally found in communities which are fearful of anger and conflict, as well as in hierarchical organizations which discourage, prohibit, and penalize open opposition.

One type of community likely to incorporate a behavior of covert opposition is one marked by "niceness." Members appear unrealistically "nice" to each other, so as to maintain a fragile unity. An unconscious collusion maintains this charade of unity and avoids conflict at all costs. Individuals in the community hold a strong but erroneous belief that alienating even one member will destroy the unity of the community. Individual members usually experience a generalized sense of impotency because they feel helpless to effect any change in the system. This impotency leads to a constant procrastination, coupled with the erroneous hope that the situation will change by itself. What passes for overt compliance is really resistance and noncompliance.

The role of the leader is to confront this covert opposition and to stimulate the members' exploration of their beliefs about conflict, opposition, and impotency. Members can be challenged to see overt opposition as a creative force rather than a destructive one.

Table 2.1 is a synthesis of the findings of Ober and Kantor for these three behavioral archetypes. We recommend that readers study this chart from a subjective, rather than objective, stance. Identify specific times when you believe the community to which you belong has engaged in each of these behaviors.

## Table 2.1

| Archetypal Behavior | Where Found | Characterized by | Recommended Response |
|---|---|---|---|
| Point-Counterpoint (move-oppose) | Highly competitive cultures | Long-standing attitude of win/lose behavior | Assertive and affirming leadership, inviting more bystanding and rewarding collaboration |
| Courteous Compliance (move-follow) | Tends to occur in traditional, hierarchical cultures that avoid confrontation with designated leaders | A milieu that is generic, bland, and rarely prophetic | Encourage "loyal" opposition |
| Covert Opposition (move-follow) or (move-bystand) | Hierarchical organizations that prohibit open opposition | Apparent overt compliance but actual resistance and non-compliance typified by an insincere, "nice" atmosphere | Explore beliefs about conflict, opposition, the futility of fighting the system, along with an encouragement of opposition |

## Summary

There are dynamics that occur between and among members in communities which either contribute to or detract from the growth and effectiveness of community. This chapter briefly explains one model for understanding some of the dynamics experienced in community. The model is predicated on the balancing of four key roles and the challenging of archetypical behaviors that have the potential to destroy community.

## Suggested Reading

Ober, Steven P. and David Kantor, "Achieving Breakthroughs in Executive Team Performance," *Prism*, Third Quarter 1996, Arthur D. Little, pp. 83-95.

## Reflection Questions

1. Identify a time when you believed the community functioned ineffectively or in a dysfunctional way. As you reflect on the material in this chapter, do you have insights as to what may have contributed to that occurrence? Can you make any recommendations about what could be done differently in the future? (Refer to Worksheet 2.A.)
2. Can you identify concrete situations in which your community has utilized all four behaviors? (Refer to Worksheet 2.B.)

## Process for Group Sharing

1. Each member complete Worksheets 2.A and 2.B.
2. Having reflected individually, share insights with the community.
3. Discuss which behaviors are encouraged and which are discouraged in your community.
4. Identify what changes in behavior you would like to make.

## Worksheet 2.A
# Dysfunctional Behavior

Identify Ineffective or
Dysfunctional Behavior

Insights as to
Cause/Dynamics

Point-Counterpoint

Courteous Compliance

Covert Opposition

# Identification of Effective Functioning

### Basic Behaviors

1. A **move** initiates a sequence of behavior.
2. A **follow** supports a move.
3. An **oppose** opposes a move.
4. A **bystand** observes and makes comments that move the group along.

| Specific Issue | Behaviors | Performed by |
|---|---|---|
| | | |

# 3
# *Beliefs About Community*

The first two chapters in Section I provide a context for understanding some normal dynamics found in all communities. The two topics addressed, the stages of community and the dynamics that occur in the interactions between members, directly affect the issues which will be raised in Section II.

Chapter 3 adds an additional dimension to this understanding of community. One of the major determinants of whether members approach community with a positive or negative attitude is the individual's beliefs about community. This chapter provides an opportunity for you to reflect on your previous communal experiences. Reflection on these experiences will help you gain clearer insights into your beliefs about community. The more consciously and clearly articulated these beliefs are, the greater the freedom and, hopefully, willingness to commit to community.

## Understanding the Genesis of Beliefs

There is a direct relationship between previous experiences in community and the beliefs one holds about community. No one enters a community with a completely unbiased attitude. Each one carries into the new situation the recollections of previous experiences. Consciously or unconsciously these experiences, positive and negative, influence attitudes, beliefs, behaviors, and consequent investment in community.

Simply put:

**Experiences** determine **Beliefs.**
**Beliefs** produce **Emotions.**
**Emotions** influence **Behavior.**

**Experiences influence your beliefs.** If your past experiences of community are positive, you have positive beliefs about the value of community. If, conversely, your recollections of community are negative, your beliefs about community and its potential for positive growth are also negative.

**Beliefs affect your emotions and feelings.** If your experiences, and therefore your beliefs, are positive you will feel hopeful and excited about the prospects of community. However, if your experiences and beliefs are negative, you will approach any community experience with fear and anxiety. Interestingly, since most people have had both positive and negative experiences, the individual is responsible for choosing which of the two experiences to focus on. This choice often happens at an unconscious level.

**Feelings determine behavior.** Those who are excited and hopeful about community will probably be more committed to expending energy in developing community. Those who are fearful and anxious will be more likely to resist serious attempts at building community. The primary behavior of the fearful, anxious people will be avoidance and even hostility.

At this point a simple but useful experience can help to personalize this paradigm. Recall an experience of community that continues to affect the way you participate in community in the present. Spend time reliving that experience. Use your memory and imagination to place yourself back in that situation and relive the experience. As a result of that experience, what beliefs have you developed about community? What emotions/feelings do those beliefs produce whenever you are encouraged to participate in community? How do those feelings influence your present behavior?

Those whose primary recollections of communal experiences are negative will not change their behavior or commit themselves to community by simple exhortation to do so. Neither will it be fruitful to cajole them into feeling excited and hopeful about the prospects of community. The one efficacious way to change their behavior is to provide them with corrective emotional experiences, i.e., positive experiences of community. As a result of having different experiences, their beliefs, feelings, and behaviors change.

It is our fervent hope and prayer that by working through the subsequent chapters, those who have developed pessimistic beliefs about community will have positive experiences of community. These corrective emotional experiences can enable a person to enjoy the positive fruits of supportive faith communities.

## Beliefs About Community

Because beliefs have a dominant effect on the continued development of community, we encourage each member to identify her or his beliefs about community. We likewise recommend that each member share these beliefs with the community. To assist in this process we have identified some of our own beliefs about community.

44

## Table 3.1
# Beliefs About Community

1. Baptismal commitment calls all Christians to community. *Called and Gifted for the Third Millennium*, published by the United States National Conference of Catholic Bishops, is a recent reaffirmation of this universal call.

2. The call to Christian community is found in the Word of God. It has its genesis in the Old Testament. The New Testament call is a continuation of the call to community identified in the Old Testament.

3. The ultimate paradigm for all Christian community is the Holy Trinity, three separate Persons in the unity of one God.

4. There is a universal hunger for community. The current trend toward individualism existing in most developing countries makes this hunger even more intense.

5. Effective Christian communities provide support, encouragement, growth, and comfort for their members.

6. Christian community differs from other communities in that it always exists for the sake of mission. Christian community is never an end in itself. It provides support for its members to engage in their Christian vocation to further the reign of God.

7. Community is a group and is subject to all the dynamics that occur in any group.

8. Community has the potential to be either a source of life and growth, or a source of destruction. The outcome is significantly determined by the community members' levels of understanding of normal group dynamics and their ability to handle those dynamics.

9. The types and forms of community are many and varied. Each community develops its own set of expectations for its members. Certain forms of community place greater demands on members and require greater levels of trust and intimacy.

10. All communities should be intentional in nature. Intentional membership requires an explicit commitment to abide by agreed upon corporate expectations.

11. Building community is difficult and messy and requires a strong commitment on the part of the members, but it is worth the effort.

# Process for Group Sharing

Three processes follow that can assist you in identifying your beliefs.

## Process 1

We invite each member to utilize Worksheet 3.A. This worksheet is designed to assist in identifying some of your major beliefs about community. We would further encourage you to identify the particular experiences that contributed to the development of those beliefs.

## Process 2

Every experience, either positive or negative, affords an opportunity for learning. This second process invites you to reflect on these positive and negative experiences and to glean the insights that can contribute to the growth of your present community.

We recommend that each member of the community spend time reflecting on the following questions (refer to Worksheet 3.B):

1. What are my most positive experiences of community? Why were they so positive? What can I learn from those experiences that might be valuable to this community?
2. What are my most negative experiences of community? Can I identify what made those experiences so negative? What is the lesson to be learned from those experiences that I would like to discuss with this community?
3. How do these positive and negative experiences influence the attitude with which I approach this community?

## Process 3

1. Select and distribute to each member a scriptural passage that projects a positive attitude about community, e.g., Matthew 18:20. Have two or three members of the community read this passage aloud with a short pause between each reading. Encourage every member to share how that passage speaks to him or her about the reality of the present community.
2. Each person is invited to share the elements that contributed to the positive experiences of community. In addition to sharing the elements, expand on what made these experiences so important.
3. Make and post a list of each of the identified elements.
4. Repeat this process for the negative elements.
5. Reflecting on the experiences shared, ask each member to express clearly, honestly, and succinctly his or her individual expectations for the community.
6. As a closing prayer, invite each member who wishes to do so to share any scripture passages regarding community that have special meaning for her or him.

# My Beliefs About Community

Belief

Experiences
That Influenced
This Belief

1.

2.

3.

4.

5.

## Worksheet 3.B
# Reflection on Experiences

| Positive<br>Experiences | Reason Why<br>Positive | Learnings/<br>Insights |
| --- | --- | --- |
| | | |

| Negative<br>Experiences | Reasons Why<br>Negative | Learnings/<br>Insights |
| --- | --- | --- |
| | | |

# Section II

# *Community Issues*

# 4

# Trust: The Cornerstone of Community

*Blessed is anyone who trusts in Yahweh.*
*—Jeremiah 17:7*

The quality of trust is an enigma in any community or in any relationship. Yet it is an enigma that must be grappled with if relationships are to develop. This is exemplified in a community that existed together for three years but was still in the stage of orientation. Characterized by a pervasive sense of mistrust, they were unable to establish a climate of safety and security. In working with the community we discovered the prime reason for the mistrust: personal material, shared during one of the early meetings, had been revealed to people outside the group. As a result some members felt betrayed. This breach of confidentiality was never discussed at any subsequent meeting, but it continued to affect profoundly the members' willingness to share openly and honestly.

Unfortunately, this example is not unique. We have encountered numerous communities where the trust level is extremely low or nonexistent. The absence of trust has a devastating effect on a community. When there is a betrayal of trust, the community is characterized by a climate of suspicion, where impersonal and guarded behavior becomes the norm. Spontaneity and personal sharing are almost completely absent. Communal growth is nonexistent until members build, or in some cases reestablish, a climate of trust.

Creating a climate of trust is one of the most important tasks of any community because trust is the essential foundation and cornerstone upon which communal relations are developed. A community will become fixated at the initial stage of orientation unless the members experience a level of trust that fosters a willingness to share.

# The Development of Trust

Trust is not a ubiquitous commodity; it is a personal response. While a climate of trust is essential, it can only occur when the members are willing to risk and to trust others in the group. Trust evolves as a slow, developmental, difficult process. To trust another is always a risk—it takes courage. There is never complete certainty that trust will be returned, so there is a hesitancy to share thoughts and feelings with others.

Community members tend to be cautious when they first come together. Giving and receiving feedback is threatening. However, it is imperative that members overcome their resistance and fear of honestly and openly sharing with others if the community is to grow and develop. It is only in this risk-taking process of self-disclosure, reception of that disclosure, and dialogue that trust blooms.

Trust is the ability to risk oneself, and there is no trust-building without risk. Sharing information about self makes one vulnerable to another, and there are no guarantees that others will receive and respect what is shared. Everyone fears rejection, ridicule, loss of respect. Allowing others into one's private space arouses fears of being hurt and manipulated. The willingness to take this risk without the absolute security of a protective safety net communicates a belief in the basic integrity of the community members. God's mandate is clear: life comes through relationship to self, to other, and to God. These relationships only mature in the crucible of trust.

Trust is not to be confused with a general cathartic purging of one's soul. Building a climate of trust takes time. When self-revelation is premature or undifferentiated, it can have an overpowering and bewildering effect. There are situations in which self-disclosure may be inappropriate and destructive. Self-disclosure is appropriate only when there is relative confidence that the vulnerability will not be exploited and that benefit rather than harm will ensue.

Each person needs to master the skills of sizing up situations and making judgments as to when it is appropriate to trust and when it is not, i.e., when, whom, and how much to trust others.

Ultimately, a climate of trust exists when members begin to express themselves without an inordinate fear of being judged and when they begin to make themselves known to others in personal ways, taking risks in community.

One of the key ingredients in the process of developing one's capacity to trust is the possession of a high level of self-esteem. Trust evolves when persons feel good enough about themselves to risk self-disclosure. Unwillingness to expose self—what one really feels and thinks—can be attributed to uncertainty about self, a weak or fragile self-esteem.

Trust is a scarce commodity in our society today. It is basically a Christian virtue. Distrust is basically unchristian. Only to the degree that individuals are able to develop relationships can they grow in the love of Christ.

In general, there are a number of things that members do to create a pervasive climate of trust. The list found in Table 4.1 can serve as a personal reflection exercise for each community member. To what degree do you see evidence of these elements in your community? Which of these elements are present in your community? Which elements are lacking or weak in your community? Which are the one or two elements that you need to work on personally?

## Table 4.1
## Elements That Help Build Trust

Willingness to progressively disclose oneself to the members of the community

Willingness to receive the disclosure of others with respect and confidentiality

Consistent behavior with others

Following through on commitments

Affirmation and acceptance of others

Avoiding judgment of others

Being trustworthy and honest

Focusing on areas that the members share in common

Scrupulously avoiding stereotypes

There are also behaviors that significantly decrease the level of trust, e.g., whenever self-disclosure is met with rejection, ridicule, disrespect, a moralistic response, or an evaluation of the disclosure. All these responses may communicate rejection.

# The Essential Need for Trust in Personal Development

Trust is an essential prerequisite for both personal and communal growth, and there is a direct relationship between the two. It is only when individuals have developed their personal ability to trust that they acquire the capacity to risk developing trust within a communal situation.

In Erik Erikson's stages of human development, Trust versus Mistrust is the first stage.[1] The subsequent stages of development are dependent on the development of this initial stage. The child develops basic trust in the first two years of life. If basic trust is not developed, the individual fails to develop the ability to trust others or to trust his or her surroundings.

53

To refuse to trust does violence to one's human personhood. It condemns a person to a life of loneliness and alienation and separates him or her from the resources for growth that God has placed in human lives.

The capacity to trust flows from an inner quality of emotional maturity that develops gradually as others help an individual discover his or her own worth. Trust increases in direct proportion to the growth in self-confidence. People act superficially to hide their feelings of inadequacy, feelings of distrust, or fear of the unknown. As they develop their capacity to trust, these kinds of reactions become less dominant.

The development of the capacity to trust makes it possible to enter into human relationships, relationships that foster personal growth. Just as the body needs food, so human beings need relationships for their personal and human development. In John Donne's words: "No man is an island of itself, each is a piece of the continent, a part of the mainland." Becoming fully human requires others in one's life. "He who says he loves only God, loves no one," Charles Peguy once said.

To build relationships, people must establish mutual trust. To trust another with the truth about oneself is the only authentic way of inviting the other to share life. Disclosing more and more thoughts, feelings, and reactions always involves some risk. The way in which the revelation is received determines whether or not there will be further sharing. When self-disclosure is met with a sense of unacceptance or a lack of validation, expect that the person doing the revealing will emotionally withdraw from the community. If there is a discernible sense of acceptance, more will be shared and trust will develop. The relationship continues to grow as both persons continue to trust and be self-disclosing.

## Trust as a Prerequisite for Community

While trust is certainly necessary for personal growth, it is also essential for the development of community. Creating a climate of trust is the most important task of a new community. The leader's responsibility is to find ways to build a climate of trust before dialogue—which is the heart of community—can begin. Constructing a trust level entails members' revealing themselves, their feelings, and their beliefs to the group. The climate of trust essential to community building cannot develop until members reach a point where they can begin to take that risk.

Early in the life of a community people tend to be closed and to program their communication carefully. They test the waters to ascertain how safe it is to trust the community with important information about themselves. Usually there is a self-revelation that is fairly non-threatening. How this is received and respected determines whether the person feels safe and comfortable enough to share additional material of a more revelatory nature.

When a climate of trust is present, the basic needs for belonging and esteem are met. Growth occurs both in the person and in the community.

## The Qualities of Trust

Trust demands the presence of a number of qualities, especially openness, sharing, and acceptance. Openness is a quality of being candid, combined with a confidence in the goodness of the other. Sharing is the willingness to be vulnerable by committing thoughts, ideas, and feelings into words. Acceptance is the quality of receiving the openness and sharing of the other.

## Openness

Openness implies two things: first, a capacity and willingness to share information, ideas, thoughts, and feelings; second, the willingness to listen intently and respectfully to others as they share these same things.

To receive trust one must begin to risk opening oneself to others. Risk and trust are the starting points for building life-giving relationships.

It takes courage to trust others with information about oneself that could eventually be used destructively. For example, if the persons trusted with confidential information reveal this inappropriately to others, one's natural response is to feel hurt, anger, and betrayal. The immediate reaction is to confront them with this response. When an individual has the courage to pursue this action, another scenario may emerge: from the perspective of the others it was not a betrayal of trust, but a sharing of truth. They acted in good faith in what they believed would be beneficial to the individual and the community. Such dialogue leads to revelations that change perceptions and beliefs, and cultivates a climate of trust.

Relate this process of openness, risk, and dialogue described in the above paragraph to the incident described in the beginning of this chapter. That community never had the openness or courage to investigate what had transpired. They became paralyzed by and victims of their fears. It was the lack of openness and dialogue that profoundly impeded the growth of trust.

Openness can be helpful or harmful, effective or ineffective, appropriate or inappropriate depending on the person's motives and ability to be sensitive to the effects of sharing on the recipient.

Trust is violated by those who are indiscriminately open without thought of their impact on others, e.g., pouring out feelings at inappropriate times or displaying insensitivity.

## Sharing

Sharing is the ability to offer insights and personal resources to others so as to move the community toward accomplishing its goal.

To share oneself with another is inviting trust, but also involves a willingness to make oneself vulnerable. Sharing is always a risk, a kind of leap in the dark with the sharer uncertain of how the others will receive and respect what is shared. Sharing often involves taking the initiative, taking the first step.

Trust develops when a member believes that the material shared has been received with a sense of respect and confidentiality. It takes an act of faith and courage to entrust personal thoughts and feelings to others since there is always the risk that what is shared will not be treated with respect and confidentiality. A community is immobilized until it reaches a point where the trust level allows group members to risk sharing.

If trust is habitually betrayed, one becomes extremely cautious of what she or he is willing to share. The lack of caution depends on the nature, severity, and frequency of the offense.

It is easier to protect the heart from hurt by not sharing, but development of our personhood is dependent on interaction with others.

### Acceptance

Acceptance is communicating to members an appreciation of who and what they are. It is a willingness to receive their sharing with respect and confidentiality. Acceptance conveys a high regard for other persons. It is a recognition of their strengths. Acceptance communicates a belief in their sacredness as a person and their value as a community member.

Expressing acceptance and support are key aspects of being trustworthy in an interpersonal relationship. Until people feel a sense of personal acceptance in the community, there will be a reluctance to share openly what is important to them and what can be beneficial to the growth of the community.

Self-acceptance is a prerequisite for acceptance of others. The more capable one is of accepting self, the greater the capacity to accept others. Defensive feelings of fear and distrust often block the development of constructive relationships. If a person does not feel accepted, the frequency and depth of disclosures will decrease.

## Summary

Trust is the foundation block for the building of community. Its absence is the clearest indication that a community is condemned to stagnation and possible dissolution.

The capacity for trust is built at both the personal and communal level. Building trust is a slow, developmental process that requires the presence of a number of elements, including openness, sharing, and acceptance.

# Suggested Readings

Hammett, Rosine and Loughlan Sofield, "Confidentiality: Some Reflections," *Sisters Today*, Nov. 1979, v. 51, #3, pp. 150-153.

Hammett, Rosine and Loughlan Sofield. *Inside Christian Community*. New York: Le Jacq Publishing, 1981, pp. 86-89.

Johnson, David. *Reaching Out*. Englewood Cliffs, NJ: Prentice-Hall, Inc., 1981.

Shea, John. *The Challenges of Jesus*. Chicago, IL: The Thomas More Association, 1984, chapter 5.

# Reflection Questions

1. How would I evaluate the level of trust in our community?
2. What behaviors and attitudes have either contributed to or detracted from developing a more positive climate of trust in our community?
3. In what ways do I personally contribute to or detract from the development of trust? How do I need to change or grow to facilitate this growth?
4. Are there specific incidents in our history as a community that continue to interfere with our ability to create a climate of trust? Are we willing to deal with them? What resources do we need to deal with them honestly and directly?

# Process for Group Sharing

1. Identify your own beliefs about trust. To the degree possible, formulate those beliefs gained from your personal experiences rather than from theoretical abstractions. Worksheet 4.A can be used to assist with this experience. Identify specific times when personal experiences have facilitated the growth of trust in your relationships and community. Also identify specific times when an experience has seriously impeded or destroyed trust. In both cases, identify beliefs you have developed as a result of these experiences.
2. Share the insights each has gained from completing Worksheet 4.A.
3. Discuss whether the insights lead to some suggested changes in attitudes or behavior that will facilitate the level of trust.
4. Are there signs of distrust that should be brought out into the open and confronted?
5. Spend time meditating on the members of your group. Take one day for each person. Reflect on their needs, their gifts, their joys, and their sorrows. Understanding often opens us to encounter the other in a new, more trusting way.

# Beliefs About Trust
## Derived from Positive and Negative Experiences

| Positive experiences of trust building | Identification of main elements in the experience | Beliefs developed as a result of the experience |
| --- | --- | --- |
| | | |

| Negative experiences of trust building | Identification of main elements in the experience | Beliefs developed as a result of the experience |
| --- | --- | --- |
| | | |

# 5
# *Membership*

*In the same way, all of us, though there are so many of us, make up one body in Christ, and as different parts we are all joined to one another.*

*—Romans 12:5*

Is everyone called to community? Theologically, the answer is clear. By virtue of baptism every Christian is called to community, i.e., to be active and contributing members of the body of Christ. The National Conference of Catholic Bishops in the United States[1] has reaffirmed the conviction of the universal call to community. However, this statement does not imply that everyone is called universally to every community. An individual's call to community is to a particular and specific community, and this differs from person to person. Each community is unique and has distinctive, defined expectations of its members. The challenge is for individuals to discern the specific community where they are called. The challenge for the community is to discern which prospective members are truly called to this community.

## Beliefs About
## Community Membership

The reflections presented in this chapter are offered to stimulate thought and discussion about community membership and to provoke individual reflection on personal beliefs about membership in community. It is hoped that this will activate discussion on the attitudes, beliefs, and realities which influence your community's acceptance of new members.

There are three extreme positions or myths concerning membership that we challenge. The first position fails to use any criteria to determine the capacity and compatibility of potential members. The second position holds that a Christian community should be all-inclusive, accepting anyone who presents himself or herself for membership. The third position restricts the understanding of "intentional community" to accept only those who display an extremely harmonious compatibility with the present members.

# Indiscriminate Acceptance of Members

Regardless of the type of community, some criteria must exist that can be used in discerning the acceptability and suitability of new members. Indiscriminate acceptance of members is counterproductive to the life of the community, as exemplified in the following story of a community of women religious.

The leadership team of an apostolic religious congregation was in the process of voting to accept the request for final vows of one of their sisters. This decision was causing them a great deal of angst. They decided to share their uncertainty in an attempt to clarify their thinking. They described a woman in her early forties who was with the congregation for almost six years. She did reasonably well in her ministry as a second grade teacher. However, she spent all her free time sequestered in her room. Behind her back community members referred to her as "the shadow," an allusion to the fact that they rarely saw her. Even when she was physically present, they could rarely engage her in dialogue. The only time she was present in any common activity was at prayers in the chapel. She rarely even shared meals with the other sisters. She refused to attend any congregation meetings because she found that these meetings provoked too much anxiety in her. As they reviewed her life in community, they asked themselves why they would even consider granting her request for final vows. The leader responded somewhat sheepishly, "But she is the first candidate we've had in a number of years."

This leader, like many community leaders, failed to ask the basic questions: "Is she called to this community?" "Does she have the capacity to live community as we understand it?" While the example used is of a religious congregation, the questions are universal and should be applied in discerning membership for any community. Each community has to determine some minimal standards and expectations for membership.

# The Prevailing Myth of All-Inclusiveness

A second myth is that a Christian community should be willing and capable of incorporating everyone who wishes to be part of that community. More intense community experiences where the members have close, daily, intimate contact, such as religious congregations, or where community is equivalent to a lifestyle, require clearer expectations and criteria than communities that assemble periodically. Not everyone is capable of living the reality of this type of community. It is not unchristian to help people discern, or to decide for them when they are incapable of making the decision, that they are not called to live an intense community life. Such a life, by virtue of its essence, places demanding expectations on its members.

We do not advocate that communities be exclusive and elitist. That would be unchristian. We do propose that if a person is incapable or unwilling to live the minimum expectations of a community, it is a clear sign that they are not called to be a member of that community. Acceptance of members who are incapable of living out these minimum requirements condemns both new members and the community to constant frustration. In addition, it results in unhealthy communities that are incapable of providing a growth-producing climate. In the example above, if the religious congregation continued to accept indiscriminately any member who applied, the result would be an erosion of both morale and effectiveness of the membership, and the withdrawal of competent members.

Everyone is called to community, but it is important to discern the type of community to which each is called.

## Intentional Communities

Recently we have heard much discussion about the concept of "intentional communities." Every community should be an intentional community, i.e., one in which the expectations for membership are clearly expressed and in which members are held accountable for those agreed upon expectations. Communities that define "intentional" in a very restrictive way, i.e., either an over-exclusive heterogeneity or a cliquish, elitist compatibility, give counter-witness. Communities that truly give gospel witness are able to grapple with the diversity that is present in most Christian communities.

The most energizing and life-giving communities are those which have been able to integrate diversity into the group. The more diversity, the greater the potential for creativity and dynamism. There was a Christian community composed of all women, who were roughly the same age, the same ethnic background, and who held very similar views on a number of significant topics such as theological orientation and cultural-societal attitudes. They developed strong affiliative bonds rather quickly. However, their sameness proved their undoing in the long run. After the initial cohesion, there was not enough diversity to generate creative responses. Although the community perdured, it lacked any vitality.

In contrast, look at another community whose membership was very diverse. The membership was composed of both women and men, spanning a wide spectrum of age range and representing a number of different cultures and races. Theologically, they also ran the gamut of convictions. Although this group struggled to develop a level of cohesiveness during the initial stages, they were committed to the group and to remaining in dialogue. It took more time and effort for them to achieve a cohesiveness, but in the long run this group was much more dynamic, effective, and mission-oriented than the first. Intentional communities that are too restrictive in allowing diversity in their membership will probably never achieve a high level of creativity, dynamism, and mission effectiveness.

# A Paradigm for Categories of Membership

We have identified four types of persons who currently exist in communities. While there is a certain artificiality about such categories, these categories can be helpful for communal reflection and discussion.

### Table 5.1
## Categories of Membership

| Category | Description | Role of Leaders and Members |
| --- | --- | --- |
| I | Gifted, called, and working at it | Support and affirm |
| II | Gifted, called, but stopped working at it and "partially defected" | Challenge to commit or to withdraw |
| III | Gifted, called, but underdeveloped | Provide opportunities for further growth |
| IV | Neither called nor gifted | Encourage to withdraw |

The first category is people who have been gifted and called into a specific community and who continue to exert the energy needed to foster the growth of that community. They believe that as members they can grow into the fullness of who God has called them to be.

In the second category are those who have also been called and gifted but have stopped contributing to the community. While they may never formally discontinue their membership in the community, for all intents and purposes they no longer participate or contribute to its growth. Too often the community, with an unrealistic sense of inclusiveness, acts as though these people are still physically and emotionally present in and committed to the community. Dr. Robert McAllister states that the community is being unfair to these people and to itself, as a community, in allowing them to exist on the periphery.[2] In fairness to them and the community, they should be invited to review their commitment. They can decide if they want to be full members with all expectations, or if not, they should be invited to leave the group.

William Meissner uses the term "partially defected" to describe this group, referring to their relationship to the community, not their personal inadequacies.[3] David Nygren and Miriam Ukeritis described these people in their study that cites some men and women religious who have migrated to the periphery of their congregation.[4] While these individuals make significant ministerial contributions, they have little to do with their communities.

Nygren and Ukeritis recommend that clearly defining boundaries and expectations will help to revitalize the community. There is a need to set minimal expectations. Anyone who can not or will not fulfill even these minimal expectations does not belong in the community.

The third category is composed of those who are gifted and called but, due to a lack of psycho-social development, have the capacity to live only a superficial communal life. If they were to achieve a higher level of maturity, they might eventually possess the potential to live a communal life. Ultimately, each individual is responsible for his or her own growth and can choose to take those steps necessary for furthering psycho-social growth. The community can only create a climate that is conducive to growth.

The fourth category encompasses those members of community who are neither gifted nor capable of meeting even the most minimal expectations. This type of person is similar to the sister described earlier in this chapter. Failure to meet at least the minimum expectations is clear evidence of the person's unsuitability for a particular community. This discernment is not a judgment of the goodness or moral character of the individual. Rather, it is a confirmation of his or her lack of call to a particular community. Membership in a community when there is no true call engenders a pervasive sense of unhappiness and unfulfillment for the individual as well as negatively affecting the climate of the community. If a community tries to integrate too many members of this fourth category, a general aura of *ennui* envelops those who are gifted, called, and attempting to live the communal expectations.

*Essential Elements* is a document in which the criteria for membership in religious congregations are delineated. Eliminate the word "religious" from the following quotation, and it provides an excellent criterion for judging the suitability of a candidate for any Christian community.

> The capacity to live (in) community with its joys and restraints is a quality which distinguishes a religious vocation to a given institute and it is a key criterion of suitability in a candidate.[5]

The four categories we have delineated, although somewhat arbitrary and artificial, provide a paradigm for determining suitable membership within any community. The categories also can be useful in determining areas of needed growth for members.

## Summary

Community can be life-giving, and it can be draining. One of the greatest drains on a community is attempting to integrate members who do not possess the desire, maturity, or gifts to participate fully in communal life. Communal growth will be enhanced if the community: (1) establishes minimum expectations with a process for accountability; (2) unearths and discusses commonly held myths about membership in community; and, (3) honestly evaluates the commitment and capacity of its members.

## Suggested Readings

Chittister, Joan, O.S.B. *The Fire in These Ashes*. Kansas City, KS: Sheed and Ward, 1995.

Corey, Gerald and Marianne Corey. *Groups: Process and Practice*. Monterey, CA: Brooks/Cole Publishing Co., 2nd ed., 1982, chapters 3, 6, and 21.

## Reflection Questions

1. Do we have clear, realistic expectations for which we hold each member accountable?
2. Is there a myth which exists among us that as a "good, Christian community" we should be able to incorporate everyone who applies for our community?
3. In what ways do we honestly evaluate the desire and capacity of an individual to live our communal life?
4. As I reflect on these four types of members, what does it say about me? About the community?

## Process for Group Sharing

1. Using Worksheet 5.A, clarify the minimum expectations each member has of anyone wishing to belong to your community.
2. Discuss your individual expectations and determine what are the common expectations that can be communicated to any new potential members.
3. Determine whether you have adequate structures for accountability regarding these expectations.
4. Assign someone to develop a list of these mutually agreed-upon expectations which can be presented to new potential members.
5. Discuss your reactions to the four categories of membership, honestly focusing on the implications for your community.

## Worksheet 5.A
# Minimal Expectations of Members

### What are the minimal expectations I have of anyone who joins this community?

1.

2.

3.

4.

*6*

# Giftedness and
# Community

*You received without charge, give without charge.*
*—Matthew 10:8*

In a television interview, the famous and world-renowned actress Angela Lansbury spoke frankly of her career as well as of her family. The interviewer asked Ms. Lansbury to expand on details of her long and successful career on both stage and screen. When asked how her career affected her family, Ms. Lansbury spoke almost tearfully of a difficult time when her children had turned to drugs and alcohol. While she was at the height of her career, successfully doing what she enjoyed, using her gifts to capacity, her children were struggling to find themselves, their value and worth as persons and their life's direction. "It was different for me and I am fortunate. It was easy for me to see my gifts. My gifts are evident in my work. Because my gifts are obvious from my work on screen and stage, they can be affirmed by others, even by people who do not know me."[1] Many people unlike Ms. Lansbury, whose gifts are not as evident as hers, may be unaware of the God-given gifts they possess. This is one of the reasons why a community is essential. It helps each person identify and acknowledge her or his gifts.

The discovery of one's giftedness is the vital response to God's call within every human person. A community is a group of individuals who come together for a mission. Each member brings gifts joining them with those of the community to carry out the mission. In this context of community, the gifts of the individual can be discovered and unwrapped.

## Beliefs About Giftedness

The first step in discovering and unwrapping gifts is identifying one's personal beliefs about the concept of gift. The following are some of our major beliefs about gifts.

67

## Table 6.1
# Beliefs About Giftedness

1. Every person is called by God and is given certain gifts.

2. All gifts are given to further the reign of God.

3. Each person is responsible to know and to develop those gifts.

4. Using one's gifts gives meaning to life.

5. Community is necessary to the knowledge of one's giftedness.

6. Gifts undergo change.

7. No one person possesses all the gifts.

8. All gifts necessary for mission are present in the community.[2]

Through their baptism, Christians are both called and gifted by God. The vocation of every Christian is a four-pronged call: to holiness, to community, to ministry/mission, and to Christian maturity.[3] Each human person is endowed by God with gifts, and it is with these gifts that Christians respond to their vocational call. Although most Christians intellectually accept this belief, the internalization of the fact often falls short. Many people struggle to think of themselves as valued and unique individuals with particular gifts that they contribute to their personal sphere in family, community, work, and ministry. The reluctance to accept oneself as a person with special gifts to offer can extend to others. There are certain individuals, types, or groups of people that everyone encounters that challenge one's belief in the universal aspect of giftedness. For whatever reason, it becomes difficult to consider these individuals as persons possessing special gifts. Instead they are viewed as people who have some human, social, material, or physical need.

For example, in a parish with a large number of house-bound elders, the pastoral council became concerned about addressing the needs of this particular group. They had identified all the services needed and had established ministries that addressed those needs. During one of their monthly meetings, a pastoral council member questioned the attitude of the council in regard to the elders in the parish. The council and other parishioners looked upon this segment of the parish only as a group who had certain identifiable needs. They challenged each other to see these house-bound elders as individuals possessing gifts that could contribute to the parish at large. In the end it was discerned with the elders that they possessed the gift of time and of prayer. Those who wished became formally installed as ministers of prayer for the parish, and each Sunday someone would bring them a list of prayer intentions for the coming week. Until the council began to take seriously the fact that *everyone* is a gifted person, the gifts of this group were denied to the larger community.

Who are the individuals in your community for whom you find this universal concept of giftedness difficult to realize and accept? Test your own attitude about the universal concept of gifts and think about a person in your community whose personality is difficult to accept, or a person with whom you find it difficult to relate. Can you recognize and name the gifts that a particular person possesses?

The gifts that God has bestowed are not just for personal enjoyment and satisfaction, but they are meant to be shared with the Christian community. The gifts that each person possesses are the vehicles provided in order to live the Christian vocation. *Called and Gifted: The American Catholic Laity* states this clearly.

> From the reception of these charisms or gifts, including those which are less dramatic, there arise for each believer the right and duty to use them in the Church and the world for the good of humankind and for the upbuilding of the Church.[4]

The Christian then, is meant to use his or her gifts by word and action in furthering the mission of the Christian community. That mission celebrates Christ's presence in the world and strives to further the reign of God. How do you encourage one another to use your gifts for the service of the mission?

With these freely dispensed gifts there comes an obligation for each person to know and to develop those gifts. This personal responsibility is emphasized by Jesus in the parable of the talents. In this story the servant who hides the one talent receives a strong rebuke for the irresponsible stewardship of that talent with the words, "You wicked and lazy servant!" (Mt 25:26). This is a strong message for every Christian. The responsibility for the gifts God has given rests on the shoulders of the receiver. With that responsibility is an accountability to develop those gifts and to discern where and how they can best be used in the service of God and others in the community.

In a world where some people experience emptiness, recognition of one's gifts can give meaning and purpose to life. The awareness of one's gifts as important and necessary to participating in extending the reign of God, and the realization that those gifts are given to help others in some way, enhances one's purpose in life.

In this discovery and acceptance of personal giftedness, the role of community is an important factor. Through reflection and self-examination, an individual can come to a limited knowledge of his or her personal gifts. However, in one's limited human view only a partial picture of the total person is visible. A more complete picture can emerge when others in the Christian community have the opportunity to surface additional gifts they have recognized, thereby helping to unwrap the many layers of giftedness that might otherwise lie dormant.

The gifts that each person possesses may change as the person experiences change over time. For example, a teacher who worked successfully with five-year-olds for many years found herself losing patience and becoming more irritable with the children. She no longer enjoyed interacting with her student class each day, but found herself looking forward to the tutoring time with the special students. As her interest in the developmentally disabled increased, she began to realize that perhaps her gift for education was changing in its focus. As a person experiences any type of life transition, it is not unusual for it to be a time when personal giftedness may be undergoing a change or development as well. As you reflect on this topic, do you find that some of your gifts have changed? Are you free to accept those changed gifts?

One of the most comforting beliefs about giftedness is that no one person embodies all the gifts. Therefore, one's personal expectations should be limited and should include the realization that one has certain gifts but does not possess others. Unfortunately, expectations can be unrealistic, and the unconscious belief that "I should possess all the gifts" becomes dominant. A person's behavior often follows that belief. As a result, he or she cannot see or admit the gifts of others, and may even prevent other community members from developing their gifts.

The complementarity and variety of gifts is the basis for community and collaboration. While no one member possesses all gifts, all the gifts necessary for carrying out the mission are present within the community.

While these belief statements are not an exhaustive list of convictions, they are a way for the reader to focus on his or her own attitude about the concept of gifts. Examining and clarifying one's own beliefs can serve as the foundation for surfacing and developing areas of personal giftedness in oneself and for sensitizing the community to the gifts that are present among the membership.

## Roadblocks in Developing Gifts

The journey into one's personal giftedness is not without obstacles and roadblocks along the way. Although the desire to discover one's gifts is real, there is generally some resistance and avoidance that prevents uncovering them completely. The blocks that keep a person from acknowledging gifts are particular to that individual, but there are five obstacles that are more common and worth noting.

## Table 6.2
# Blocks to Identifying and Developing Gifts

1. False or misplaced notion of humility
2. Perception that a gift is commonplace or ordinary
3. Belief that one's gift is possessed universally by everyone
4. Envy of another's gifts
5. Fear

The first such obstacle is a misplaced notion of humility. Through culture or family background, there can be an inbred tendency to minimize or diminish one's positive qualities or abilities. It is as though by denying God-given gifts and attributes, one is practicing the virtue of humility. On the contrary, one's abilities, talents, and qualities are gifts and as such should be seen as a reason for praising God's goodness. This does not imply that boasting or self-aggrandizement is an appropriate or acceptable response to one's personal giftedness. True humility acknowledges the gift knowing that its source is a gracious and generous God.

The next block does not allow a gift to be acknowledged because it seems commonplace or ordinary. The misconception that all gifts have to be spectacular can prevent a person from accepting them. When the expectation for a gift is set too high, the "ordinary gifts" such as listening, compassion, mirth, hospitality, which enrich human life, can be easily overlooked.

The presumption that one's gifts are possessed universally by everyone and, therefore, are not worthy of acknowledgment is the third roadblock in discovering personal giftedness. A senior citizen who was participating in a gift discernment process struggled to identify the gifts she offered to her community. When the group affirmed her gift of approachability, she shrugged it off, saying, "Oh, everyone has that gift." The group was quick to challenge her, pointing out that, if it were true, then why were so many people drawn to specifically contact her when they needed advice or consolation. Their appreciation of her gift led the woman to an awareness that she was in possession of a gift that not everyone else had.

Envy of another's gifts is the fourth obstacle. While it may be a challenge to see the gifts within self, it may be easier sometimes to focus on the gifts that others possess. Obvious and prominent gifts may become the object of one's desire, and much energy is spent on coveting another's gift. Several years ago the popular film *Amadeus* epitomized vividly the face of envy in the person of the musician and composer Salieri. A gifted musician and composer in his own style, Salieri became oblivious to his own talent and so obsessed with Mozart's gift for musical composition that his jealousy and envy destroyed both himself and Mozart. While most people will not envy another to such an extreme, wasting energy focusing on those gifts one does not have detracts from discovering and developing the gifts one does possess.

The fifth and final area of resistance is fear. This can be an especially difficult block to overcome because the root of the fear may be many-faceted. The identification of certain gifts will be accompanied by a challenge to use those gifts. This can trigger a fear of becoming overwhelmed and overcommitted, and of moving in too many directions at the same time. This need not occur since surfacing certain gifts may mean letting go of others, or rechanneling or refocusing those still needed. For some, the fear can arise from feelings of uncertainty or insecurity as to one's ability to develop the newly discovered gift. Another dimension can be the fear that discerning one's gifts may demand changes in life. These changes could appear in attitude, behavior, activities, ministry, work, or even lifestyle. The normal resistance to change that everyone experiences may be accentuated at this juncture and may make overcoming this fear particularly difficult.

The presence of obstacles can create an inertia that deters a person from the ongoing discovery and acceptance of God-given gifts. It is beneficial before entering into a gift discernment process to reflect on the personal roadblocks that may prevent freely accepting God's gifts.

## Categories of Gifts

The word *gift* has a generic ring to it that, in itself, can create a hesitancy about discerning one's gifts. It may prove useful to consider gifts in three categories: gifts of faith experiences, natural gifts, and gifts from life's experiences. Though this is not an all-inclusive list of categories, it can provide a framework when one sits down prayerfully to discern his or her gifts.

One's faith life provides an area of giftedness that is frequently overlooked, yet it is rich in gifts. Those quiet times in prayer when there is a sense of God's love, a grace experienced, an insight received, a contemplative moment, are gifts arising from one's faith life and relationship with God. As gifts are meant to be shared, these faith experiences are to be reflected on and shared with others so that the faith of the community can be enhanced.

Categorized as natural gifts are all those abilities, qualities, talents, and skills that comprise who we are as unique human beings. These gifts change, develop, and expand as a person grows and matures over a lifetime. They are characteristic of each individual. When one employs a natural gift, there is a sense of enjoyment and comfortableness. There are the ordinary and simple gifts of life: spontaneity, warmth, hospitality, approachability, gentleness, humor, compassion, ability to listen, artistic ability, leadership, generosity, mechanical ability, scholarship, kindness, insightfulness, to name just a few. The natural gifts might be forgotten or minimized because they are so very much a part of one's person.

Throughout everyone's life, innumerable experiences each leave an imprint in some form. The third area of giftedness emerges from the many aspects of life's experiences: formal (education and training) and informal (passages through crises and encounters with God). Particularly noteworthy are the experiences that have inflicted trauma on the human spirit. Through those situations and encounters which are usually accompanied by pain and suffering, one often finds that some ability or quality emerges as a result. These unexpected gifts from God can be shared with others experiencing similar trauma. This is the working principle of Alcoholics Anonymous. Individuals who have battled their disease of alcoholism generously reach out to assist and to accompany others who are still struggling to overcome their addiction.

Another example of this type of gift can be found in the story of a young woman who had recently undergone a painful divorce. It necessitated her changing jobs, relocating herself and her children to another city, establishing another residence, and reacclimatizing herself and her children to a new life. She joined a prayer group in her new parish and began to establish new relationships. A member of her new community was anticipating a divorce. Knowing the pain and anguish of that experience, the woman extended herself to the other person, offering support, advice, and encouragement. Her continued faithfulness to God's presence in her life during her own experience gave her a gift she shared with the other community member. What are the experiences in your own life that have been the vehicle for God's giving you a new gift? What is the gift and how are you called to share it with others?

## Summary

The discovery of one's giftedness is a vital response to God's call within every human person. Each person is a storehouse of gifts placed there by God. These gifts can be natural abilities, talents, qualities, characteristics, and skills. In community, gifted individuals join together toward a common mission. Each member of the community contributes the gifts received personally. While the desire to realize one's giftedness exists, there is also a resistance to discovering those gifts. All obstacles need to be reviewed so as not to stand in the way of developing one's gifts. One way of coming to a fuller knowledge of gifts is to discern three types: those from faith experiences, those which are natural gifts, and those from life experiences. A process for discerning gifts provides an opportunity for individuals to discover the unique and beautiful ways God has enriched them. This discernment also gives people a heightened awareness that their giftedness is the way they respond to their vocation as Christians.

## Suggested Readings

National Conference of Catholic Bishops. *Called and Gifted: The American Catholic Laity*. Washington, DC: United States Catholic Conference, 1980.

National Conference of Catholic Bishops. *Called and Gifted for the Third Millennium: Reflections of the U.S. Catholic Bishops on the Thirtieth Anniversary of the Decree on the Apostolate of the Laity and the Fifteenth Anniversary of Called and Gifted*. Washington, DC: NCCB/USCC, 1995.

Padovani, Martin H. *Healing Wounded Emotions*. Mystic, CT: Twenty-Third Publications, 1990, pp. 107-113.

Ripple, Paula. *Growing Strong at Broken Places*. Notre Dame, IN: Ave Maria Press, 1986, pp. 117-128.

## Reflection Questions

1. What are the obstacles or roadblocks that prevent you from recognizing and accepting your gifts?
2. How does the climate in your community encourage and affirm the differing gifts of its members?
3. Which are the gifts in community members that are most difficult for you to acknowledge and affirm? Why?

## Process for Group Sharing

The community participates in a gift discernment process. This process can be used when the community has been together a sufficient time for the members to know each other fairly well.

Since the process requires that each member discern his or her gifts individually, it may be repeated on several occasions. This will allow one or two members to share their gifts at each session depending on the length of the session and the number in community.

### Gift Discernment Process

1. Set the climate and allow sufficient time for sharing of gifts. Each person spends some time with a passage of scripture relating to gifts, such as:

   Ex 34:4; 36:7             Mt 25:14-30, 31-36
   Rom 8:14-17; 12:1-8       1 Cor 12:4-11, 12-26
   Eph 3:14-21, 4:1-16       Jn 6:5-15; 8:31-36; 15:1-11
   Rom 12:1-8

2. Allow each person to share his or her beliefs about gifts.
3. Ask each person to write a list of his or her gifts. Next, focus on the other members in the gift discernment process and draw up a list of gifts you see in them or want to affirm.

4. The community regathers and each person in turn will share his or her gifts. One person begins by reading her or his list and then quietly listens as other members offer a response.

5. Each member is invited to respond to the person's gifts in a specific and concrete way by:
   a) *affirming* those gifts he or she has experienced by offering specific examples;
   b) *questioning or challenging* those gifts that he or she does not believe the person possesses and offering other gifts in their place;
   c) *adding* gifts not mentioned by the person but which have been observed by the community;
   d) *applying* how the gift might be used in the community or in response to a need in the larger Christian community.

6. This procedure is repeated for each member of the group.

7. After all have had the opportunity to experience this gift-sharing, a celebratory, prayerful response closes the session.

8. The community is reminded that all the information shared is confidential to the community who participated in the gift discernment process.

# 7
# *Conflict:*
# *Embrace or Avoid?*

*There was sharp disagreement so that they parted company, and Barnabas sailed off with Mark to Cyprus.*

*—Acts 15:39*

Each of us is a word of God spoken only once. Each member of a community is unique. In diversity lies strength but also challenge. This diversity provides the potential for growth but frequently results in conflict. Conflict is bound to arise in all relationships and in every group. When recognized, addressed, and embraced, conflict contributes to the growth of relationships and community. When avoided, conflict becomes a cancerous organism draining life from a community.

## Conflict as a Normal Reality in the Life of Every Community

Conflict is a predictable stage in the life of every community. It is universal, inevitable—and as old as humankind. The word "conflict" comes from the Latin *conflictus*, meaning "striking together." In this "striking together," there is potential for progress as well as disaster, for growth as well as destruction. The issue is not the existence of conflict, but the way in which it is addressed. Often there is a powerful, at times unconscious, collusion among community members to ignore conflict. When this occurs, it precipitates either apathy or intense tension and the eventual erosion or demise of the community.

Conflict is a normal aspect of genuine relationships. It begins when our needs, wants, values, and ideas clash with the needs, wants, values, and ideas of others. Each individual has a need to be loved and affirmed, to be understood and to belong. In attempting to have these needs met in community, members experience tension and conflict.

77

Conflict will arise, but it can be addressed in such a way that members experience respect, compassion, and understanding—qualities which draw them into the group rather than alienate them.

A community cannot become a cohesive, supportive, nurturing community until it is able to deal directly and effectively with conflict. Unresolved conflict hangs like a dark cloud over the group, boding disaster. The specter of disaster often results in the group's grasping at any reasonable rationale to run from the conflict and avoid it. To deny its existence is to condemn the community to stagnation and death. Growth takes place when people are free to look at a situation from different angles and acknowledge the value of each angle. In dialogue, different points of view emerge and the potential for growth escalates for all concerned parties.

When conflict is faced, it can reduce the natural tension and frustration people experience as they work together. Unfortunately, many communities feel they are incapable of handling conflict and seek ways to avoid it. To the extent that a community is willing to acknowledge and address conflict, the level of alienation experienced by the members will decrease significantly.

## Conflict as a Christian Reality

It is unfortunate when Christians assume that conflict is "unchristian." While it is not unchristian to experience conflict, it can be unchristian to deny or refuse to confront it. The scriptures are replete with the seemingly ever-present conflicts that occurred in the early church. Conflict is inevitable in the Christian community.

Conflict, in and of itself, is neither good nor bad. Jesus, for instance, did not shun conflict. He was often surrounded by it and enmeshed in it. He challenged the religious establishment of his time by healing on the sabbath and ended up embroiled in a conflict with them that cost him his life.

The gospel story of the disciples on the way to Capernaum is a wonderful example of the conflict present in the early Christian community. The gospel of Mark (9:33-34) contains the story of the conversation that took place on this journey: "They came to Capernaum, and when he got into the house he asked them, 'What were you arguing about on the road?' They said nothing, because on the road they had been arguing which of them was the greatest." Even among the followers of Christ there were tensions and jealousies. Here is a case of power and esteem: who was closest to the Master; who counted most? Jesus was aware that conflict is a part of every relationship. He did not reprimand them for their conflict, but rather for their ambition.

In Galatians (2:11) Saint Paul opposed Cephas to his face on the matter of circumcision. The incident is developed more fully in the Acts of the Apostles and is described as a "disagreement" that led to "a long argument" between Paul and Barnabas and the group who held the opposing view (Acts 15:2).

Also in the same chapter of Acts, "Barnabas suggested taking John Mark, but Paul was not in favor of taking along the man who had deserted them in Pamphylia and had refused to share in their work. There was sharp disagreement so that they parted company, and Barnabas sailed off with Mark to Cyprus" (15:37-39).

In another instance of conflict, Paul confronts Peter when Peter breaks off his table fellowship with the Gentile Christians in Antioch (Gal 2:11-14). According to Paul, the unity of the church was at stake because of Peter's conduct. In breaking off table relationship, Peter sets up opposition between Jews and Greeks. Paul stubbornly defended the freedom of Gentile Christians from the law. "There can be no longer Jew nor Greek, there can be neither slave nor freeman" (Gal 3:28). There is only full equality in the realm of the community.

Conflict in the Christian community did not cease with the ending of the apostolic period. Church history, right down to the present day, is replete with the stories of bitter disputes and conflicts.

In 155 AD Saint Polycarp, the bishop of Smyrna, had a disagreement with Pope Amicetus about the right date for celebration of Easter. Eusebius, an early church historian, describes the conflict in which both men disagreed with one another, but their approach to the conflict offers a model of how, in spite of their differences, they parted in peace.

The church has a rich history of conflict that reaches into the present day.

## Conflict as a Difficult but Constructive Process

Conflict, although always difficult and usually painful, can be a creative and energizing force. As noted in earlier chapters, one's beliefs and belief systems play a key role in how one approaches any issue. Table 7.1 identifies some of our beliefs about conflict.

### Table 7.1
### Beliefs About Conflict

1. Conflict is inevitable in any human relationship.

2. There are a number of different causes of conflict.

3. Conflict is a difficult dynamic to acknowledge.

4. Conflict can be destructive or constructive.

5. The process used to deal with conflict may be more important than the decisions reached.

6. Conflict resolution differs from conflict management.

7. Change in one part of a system can affect and cause conflict in all other parts.

8. There are learnable skills for handling conflict.

9. The fear of conflict is often more destructive than the conflict itself.

We encourage you to reflect on your beliefs and the genesis of those beliefs. Worksheet 7.A is designed to help you do that.

# Essential Elements of Conflict

Personal and shared beliefs form one's basic attitude and approach toward conflict. In addition, there are other elements that can positively influence one's view of conflict. Chief among these elements are personal reflection, dialogue, and action.

## Personal Reflection

Conflict becomes growth-producing when we are willing to investigate personally our needs, values, feelings, and personal histories.

Self-reflection leads to self-awareness. Knowledge of self—one's reactions, needs, values, feelings, and vulnerabilities—can place a person in a position of openness to others. When this is true, there is less need to be defensive, even when what is being said is personally threatening. In the absence of threat, there is a freedom to explore every aspect of the conflict and one's role in it.

Personal awareness does not come easily, nor do we mean to imply that personal awareness leads to a sense of comfort with conflict. Conflict is messy. The immediate and almost spontaneous reaction of most healthy people is to distance themselves from conflict. However, the more healthy and mature people are, the more their initial emotional reaction of flight is replaced by the intellectual conviction that avoidance will only exacerbate the problem.

Another normal reaction to conflict is to shift the focus onto others rather than on one's self. To focus on others is much less anxiety-producing than focusing on self.

> People in conflict focus more on others than on themselves. When anxiety is high, they blame and criticize others, project their own problems on others, fight and become abusive.[1]

Engaging in self-reflection in the midst of conflict is extremely difficult because the anxiety created by conflict triggers one's personal defense mechanisms. Kelly advocates that, although self-reflection is difficult, it is essential. The reflection itself can reduce anxiety and allow one to deal with the conflict.

> It takes two to fight—and both . . . need to be anxious, whether that anxiety expresses itself as criticism or defensiveness. Calm and thoughtful people are not critical and not other-focused. The task, then, for the critical person is to pray for calm, thoughtful reflection on self.[2]

## Dialogue

Reflection should lead to dialogue. Dialogue can lead to growth, but it can also create stress. On the positive side, mutual sharing of expectations, doubts, and fears leads to a discovery of similarity. In listening to one another, there is a growing appreciation and valuing of the other. However, given the diversity existing in any group, this same dialogue magnifies the differences and diverse points of view that exist, often precipitating further conflict.

Given this potential for conflict, some people choose to forgo dialogue. This avoidance has severe repercussions. To withhold oneself from others locks a person into ignorance of one's deepest self. As anxiety-producing as conflict is, when embraced, it can lead to valuable self-knowledge. Self-knowledge comes only through relationship. Yet any close relationship will be subject to stress, tension, and conflict. Dialogue requires trusting and sharing, taking the risks of self-disclosure with its potential for conflict. Failure to share oneself with others can condemn a person to loneliness.

Sharing often results in the overcoming of individual fears and the acknowledgment of mutual needs and interdependency. Such a climate facilitates the ability to deal with diversities more constructively.

Dialogue closes the space between human persons. This is its power, its attraction, and its threat. Being close increases the potential for intimacy as well as the possibility of conflict and confrontation.

Discussing different points of view can lead to understanding and insight. As a result, a stronger community can be cultivated and all members benefit. When differences are faced, the group can use greater creativity in facing problems. The challenge is to discover ways to profit from differences rather than be divided by them.

## Action—Dealing with Conflict

Reflection and dialogue are not enough. They should lead to action: choices to confront the issues that cause the conflict, and decisions about how to establish a climate that will be conducive to positive action steps.

Inability, or more likely unwillingness, to work through conflict accounts for the breakup of many communities. The greater the awareness of the anticipated conflict, the greater the possibility that it will be dealt with constructively.

Unexpected situations of conflict generate automatic responses and defensive reactions that interfere with clear thinking, listening, and speaking. Consequently, perceptions are frequently inaccurate. Because of the presence of "repetition compulsion" (the tendency to react repetitively and consistently in the same manner), each community often assumes a predictable response. Following in Table 7.2 are some of the more common responses. Which response do you and your community generally use? Is that the most healthy response? Which response do you believe would be the healthier?

## Table 7.2
# Possible Responses to Conflict

1. Ignore it: refuse to acknowledge its existence.
2. Even when aware of it, refuse to see it as a problem, as *our* problem.
3. Avoid it because we fear it.
4. Acknowledge its existence but refuse to take any personal responsibility for it.
5. Acknowledge its existence but engage in behavior that trivializes and minimizes it, such as changing the subject or taking refuge in humor.
6. Face it honestly and deal with it courageously, trusting in the Spirit and in one another.

Our bias is rather transparent. The healthiest response is number six: to face it and deal with it. It is not the conflict, as we have repeatedly cautioned, but rather the avoidance of conflict that is destructive to community. Conflict allows for the constructive expression of aggressive feelings that, denied or avoided, surface in ways which interfere with the quality of communal life.

Members feel good when they learn to interact in a confrontative, non-defensive, nonjudgmental manner. In general, there are many conditions that contribute to conflict's becoming a positive experience. A number of these are listed in Table 7.3.

## Table 7.3
# Conflict Becomes a Positive Experience When . . .

It motivates you to draw on untapped abilities and develop new skills.

It encourages you to find new ways to deal with problems.

It stimulates your interest in community and in one another.

It forces you to clarify your views or reexamine your positions.

It promotes personal growth.

It clears the air and brings you closer to others.

Denise Carmody provides us with an appropriate paradigm for dealing with conflict in Christian communities. "In the essence of the faith, unity; in doubtful matters, freedom; and in all matters, charity."[3]

Table 7.4 offers some general principles valuable in dealing with conflict.

**Table 7.4**
# General Principles for Dealing with Conflict

1. Acknowledge the presence of the conflict. The persons involved must realize and indicate to themselves and to each other that a conflict is taking place. As simple and logical as this sounds, it does not occur often enough.

2. Help everyone become aware of his or her role in the conflict. Everyone involved in the conflict must be brought to see objectively the nature, character, and implications of his or her own position.

3. Assist everyone to understand the position of the other. Every member must be helped to see objectively the nature and implications of the other person's position.

4. Seek a resolution that does not leave anyone feeling victimized. It would be wonderful if this were always possible, but it is not. To the degree that it is possible, attempt to arrive at a resolution that is reasonable, advantageous, or at least acceptable to the parties involved.

5. Clarify what is ambiguous. Ambiguity breeds conflict. Attempt to clarify whatever causes ambiguity: language, meanings, expectations, beliefs, points of view, etc. Employ whatever means are necessary to improve the level of communication and comprehension.

6. Be sensitive to the capacity of the members to tolerate conflict. The duration and intensity of the conflict must be matched to the capability of the involved parties.

7. Help people be realistic. Not all conflicts can be resolved. Tension and conflict are a normal part of Christian community. Sometimes the best we can hope for is conflict management.

8. Encourage the participants to be forgiving. Forgiveness is at the heart of the caring community. We are all wounded persons, and, consciously or unconsciously, we can and do hurt each other. It is the not the absence of forgiveness that must characterize the Christian community, but the presence of forgiveness. Forgiveness is the focus of chapter eight.

In a previous book, *Collaborative Ministry*, we offered some additional advice for dealing with conflict.

## Conflict Management

While the ideal is to resolve the conflict and have everyone go away relieved and satisfied, this is a rare conclusion. The best that can be hoped for is management of the conflict, meaning that there is still disagreement, but because of a higher value, such as the common mission, the community continues to function as community. While the word "conflict" refers to the struggle or clashing of views or statements, conflict management involves diagnosing the nature of the conflict and using cooperative methods to move into the problem-solving stage. Management requires some "give" on each side with the objective of continuing to function together as a community.

Here the greater good depends on the ability to work together rather than to "win." It consists of honestly placing the facts as one perceives them before others, of bringing ideas together for comparison, of extending an invitation for objective examination of the facts.

Conflict management can result in group cohesion whereas avoiding the conflict results in a loss to all parties. Conflict that is not managed does not just go away but rather remains as an invisible barrier that results in pain and loss for all involved.

## Summary

Each person is unique. The strength of community lies in its diversity. As members share, they become aware of similarities and differences, hopes and fears. It is these that can produce conflict. Through conflict, these diversities can become a meaningful part of a genuine relationship of members. It is not unchristian to experience conflict. Instead, denial of conflict and refusal to confront it are unchristian. Conflict becomes a source of growth when a community does not allow its presence to manipulate them into denial or avoidance but rather deals with it against a background of respect, compassion, and understanding. Conflict must be embraced, not avoided.

## Suggested Readings

Mueller, William and Bill Kell. *Coping With Conflict*. New York: Appleton-Century-Crofts, 1972.

Sofield, Loughlan, S.T., and Carroll Juliano, S.H.C.J. *Collaborative Ministry: Skills and Guidelines*. Notre Dame, IN: Ave Maria Press, 1987, pp. 101-116.

Woodward, Evelyn. *Poets, Prophets and Pragmatists*. Notre Dame, IN: Ave Maria Press, 1987, pp. 135-176.

# Reflection Questions

1. What scares you most when conflict arises in community?
2. How was conflict handled in your family? How did you handle conflict when you were growing up?
3. Is there a high enough level of trust in your community to deal with conflict?
4. What skills do you (individually and communally) need in order to handle conflict better?
5. Are we mature enough to bring in whatever resources are needed to deal more effectively with conflict?

# Process for Group Sharing

## Process 1

1. Use Worksheet 7.B to track recent experiences of conflict in the community.
2. Invite the members to discuss the following questions:
   - Do we believe that dealing with conflict is important? Why?
   - As I reflect on my responses to Worksheet 7.A, what insights does it provide me about our community?
   - What are the fears and other obstacles which prevent us from dealing more directly and effectively with conflict?
   - What steps do we need to take to deal more effectively with conflict?
3. After the next meeting, take time to see what conflicts were present and to evaluate how we addressed them.

## Process 2

Every person has a preferred mode of behavior when faced with conflict. For a change of pace, turn to the animal world for a view of how different animals manage the conflict in their lives.

Worksheet 7.C offers some animal caricatures that might typify how you view conflict in your life. Have some fun with the exercise. Check the one or ones that are similar to you. Remember, of course, that caricatures are exaggerated and ridiculous.

# Worksheet 7.A

Beliefs About Conflict

Events That Influenced
Those Beliefs

1.

2.

3.

4.

## Worksheet 7.B
# Tracking Recent Experiences of Conflict

Experiences        How We Handled It        Other Ways to Handle It

# Animals in Conflict

| | |
|---|---|
| The Ostrich | If I hide my head, it will go away. |
| The Mother Hen | I have to protect everybody so no one will get hurt. |
| The Lion | I have to rule the jungle; they'll listen if I roar. |
| The Dove | I have to keep the peace, so I'll agree with anything. |
| The Roadrunner | I cannot take it; I'm out of here. |
| The Turtle | I'll pull my head in and withdraw. |
| The Fox | I'll be sly and jump in, surprise them and get my way. |
| The Snake | I'll sting them with my venom. |
| The Shark | When I see blood, I'll go for the jugular. |
| The Greyhound | I'll follow the rabbit around; she or he has the right idea, I'll take her or his side. |
| The Elephant | I'm big and powerful. If I don't get my way I'll trample on them. |
| The Parrot | If I keep talking and repeating myself, maybe it will all go away. |

Can you add other animals that might symbolize your stance toward conflict?

# Discussion

1. Each member of the community shares which animal(s) typifies his or her stance toward conflict and why.
2. What animals would you use to describe each other's reactions toward conflict?
3. Reflect together on what this humorous exercise says about your reactions to conflict.
4. Are there changes you would like to initiate as to how you manage conflict in your life?

# 8

# *Forgiveness: The Life of Community*

*Jesus said, "Father forgive them; they do
not know what they are doing."*
—*Luke 23:34*

Pope John Paul II, in his encyclical, *Redemptoris Missio*, states, "Two gestures are characteristic of Jesus' mission: healing and forgiving."[1] These two traits should characterize every follower of Jesus and be the hallmark of any Christian community. This chapter focuses on forgiveness, a difficult but essential attribute for the growth and development of community.

## Understanding Forgiveness

In a world of flawed communication, community is possible only through understanding others. In a world of painful alienation, community is created by accepting others. In a world of broken trust, community is sustained by forgiveness.

For all Christians, there is a call and a responsibility to forgive, to seek reconciliation with self, with God, and with others. This Christian imperative to forgive others as God has forgiven is not a simplistic act completed only once, but a multifaceted response with many dimensions. Forgiveness wears many faces:

## Table 8.1
# The Many Faces of Forgiveness

Forgiveness is restoration and reconciliation.

Forgiveness demands that we view others through the eyes of mercy.

Forgiveness restores what has been damaged and brings healing where there has been alienation.

Forgiveness restores unity where there has been division.

Forgiveness attempts to foster reconciliation where oneness ceases to exist.

Forgiveness is right relationships with God and neighbor.

Forgiveness means loving genuinely with a love that goes beyond the problem and extends to the person(s) involved.

Forgiveness demands a well-developed level of maturity.

Forgiveness comes slowly. When the injury is deep, layers are peeled back gently, compassionately, and slowly.

Forgiveness is never easy.

"Forgive and forget." Though a classic admonition, it is rarely helpful and often harmful. Painful memories of the past are never completely expunged, so the task is to refuse to let those memories control and unduly influence one's behavior in the present. Holding on to anger and resentment is paralyzing. It retards growth and interferes with one's capacity to grow as a loving person. On the other hand, forgiveness creates freedom to move into the newness of life. Lewis Smedes has described this process accurately, "The test of forgiving lies with healing the lingering pain of the past, not with forgetting that the past ever happened."[2]

## Reasons for Forgiving

There are many valid reasons to choose forgiveness as a response to hurt or injury. Two of note are theological and personal.

Some of the most compelling theological reasons were articulated, surprisingly, in *Time* magazine. This secular magazine reported on Pope John Paul II's visit in jail with Mehmet Ali Agca, the man who shot him. The *Time* authors in a series of challenging statements articulate sound theological reasons for forgiveness. In describing the Pope's action they declared, "This startling drama of forgiveness and reconciliation was not just a private act, but was also a message to the world," a witness to the essence of Christianity.

The writers challenged their readers by recalling that forgiveness is not a normal human reaction: to err is human, to forgive divine. The choice to forgive another reflects Jesus who forgave his enemies from his cross.

*Time* declared that loving one's enemies is at the "center of the New Testament." To forgive one's enemies was a constant message of Jesus Christ. To hold forgiveness as a value distinguishes Christians from many other religions and cultures.

*Time* continued: "Forgiveness is actually a profound transaction. It is the working model for human relationship with God. . . . Not to forgive is to condemn oneself to a stuttering repetition of evil."

It may seem strange that these powerful theological reasons for forgiveness were detailed in a secular news magazine. However, the concept of forgiveness is increasingly presented in the so-called secular media. The television news magazine "20/20" recently produced a segment extolling the value of forgiveness and indicating that "forgiveness therapy" has had phenomenal success. Among the comments made by the reporters Hugh Downs and Deborah Roberts was the following:

> Studies show that letting go of anger and resentment can reduce the severity of heart disease, and in some cases, even prolong the lives of cancer patients. Overall, it seems forgiveness may be one way to a healthier life.[3]

And we would add, to a healthier community.

The Psychology Department of the University of Wisconsin, in a published report of a study they conducted, challenges every Christian by stating,

> Interpersonal forgiveness in Christianity is to be strictly analogous to the divine form. . . . As one is forgiven, he or she must practice forgiveness toward others. . . . The forgiver, too, experiences peace.[4]

The study tracks an understanding of forgiveness through a variety of cultures and religions and concludes that forgiveness is a uniquely Christian value.

In addition to theological reasons, there are numerous practical considerations that support forgiveness.

## Table 8.2
# Practical Reasons for Forgiveness

1. Forgiveness is a benefit to emotional health. Anger is an extremely painful emotion. It can also be self-destructive when it is expressed in a harmful and injurious way. A community frozen in unforgiven anger is a community where the Spirit is unable to bring life.

2. Forgiveness is a factor in physical wellness. Anger produces excessive amounts of glandular secretions in the body. These secretions can ultimately cause many physical problems, e.g., heart attack, stroke, ulcers, and even death.

3. Forgiveness helps a person live fully in the present. By choosing to nurse past injuries and hurts and clutching the desire for revenge, a person condemns himself or herself to the past. The joy, beauty, and profit of daily life is absent.

4. Forgiveness gives a person control over life. When one's emotional response is altered by recalling a person who has inflicted pain, then one's emotional life is controlled by that person. Forgiveness frees the forgiver from the control of another.

5. Forgiveness is primarily a gift to oneself. As a by-product of giving forgiveness to another, the gift of new life is received.

## Obstacles to Forgiveness

As stated earlier, making the choice to forgive another presents a difficult situation. An initial phase in the process is an honest appraisal of one's personal reasons for having chosen to hold on to anger. Worksheet 8.A provides an opportunity to personalize the obstacles to forgiveness.

One of the major obstacles in building community is the inability, or more accurately, the unwillingness, of the members to forgive each other for the real or imagined hurts of the past. Why do you hold on to anger, hostility, resentment, and grudges? Why do you refuse to offer to self and others the gift of forgiveness?

There are situations and individuals that can make it more difficult to forgive, e.g.,

- those who are at a geographical distance or are no longer part of our lives;
- people who do not care whether or not we forgive them;
- those who are unaware that they have caused us pain;
- people whose actions appear to be too evil to be forgiven;
- those who are not known to us but whose actions have caused us hurt.

To add to the difficulties, many people discover that they have more trouble forgiving themselves than forgiving others. The lack of self-forgiveness often precludes the ability to forgive others. Some find it easier to forgive others and self than to forgive God. While some are fortunate enough to acknowledge their anger at God, for others even admitting such feelings would produce an inordinate amount of anxiety and guilt. These are often the people who have the most difficult time with forgiveness.

Another obstacle to consider is the absence of models of forgiveness in one's life: the lack of personal witnesses to the fullness of Christian forgiveness serves as an added impediment.

## Models of Forgiveness in Our Own Time

Besides the example of Pope John Paul II noted earlier, there are other outstanding present-day models. On a recent trip to El Salvador, we visited the bungalow where Oscar Romero lived. It is just a short three-minute walk from the chapel where he was murdered. In the front room of the bungalow is a closet. Hanging in that closet, clearly visible behind a glass door, are the shirt and alb which Romero was wearing when he was shot. There is a small, almost imperceptible, hole in the chest area of the alb and shirt. The hole could easily be mistaken for a tiny, unmended rip, but it shows the entry point of the bullet that ended the life of this modern-day saint. The alb with Romero's dried blood caked on it in rust-colored blotches remains as a poignant symbol of the profound witness to the life and death of this exceptional man. Transfixed by these haunting reminders of this terrible atrocity, we recalled the words of this selfless saint, which he uttered just two weeks before his death, "You can tell them, if they succeed in killing me, that I pardon them."[5]

Archbishop Romero echoes the prayer of forgiveness uttered by Jesus just prior to his death on the cross, "Father, forgive them for they know not what they do." Both Jesus and Romero proclaim forgiveness for those who savagely take their lives.

However, it was not only the story of this martyred prelate which had such a profound impact on us during the visit. We heard countless stories of many other Salvadoran people who offered a similar witness of divine forgiveness. These were the people whose families, friends, and neighbors had been murdered during the violent, blood-filled times in this Central American country. These individuals, like Romero, challenge all of us to look at the place of forgiveness in our lives. Most people will not experience the extreme tragedies and losses that were part of the lives of the Salvadoran people, but sometimes it seems equally challenging to forgive even the relatively inconsequential offenses in one's life.

Another profound witness of forgiveness is Joseph Cardinal Bernardin of Chicago. Three years prior to his death, Cardinal Bernardin was publicly accused of sexual abuse by a young man dying of AIDS. Bernardin later talked about how devastating this accusation had been for him. When the young man was close to death, Bernardin flew to his bedside to forgive him personally for the erroneous accusation and to attempt reconciliation. Msgr. Kenneth Velo, who preached Bernardin's eulogy, praised the Cardinal for his extraordinary act of virtue and quoted from the prayer of St. Francis, asserting that Bernardin knew that "it is in pardoning that we are pardoned."

Take time now to reflect on the people who have witnessed forgiveness for you. Be specific about where and when you have seen that witness (see Worksheet 8.A).

## Stages in the Process of Forgiveness

Authentic forgiveness cannot be forced. The journey to forgiveness is usually a long, arduous one requiring commitment, persistence, and grace to overcome one's resistance, doubt, fear, and painful brokenness. Christians sometimes attempt to rush people to forgiveness. Failure to proceed through the painful and slow process simply produces a pseudo-forgiveness in which the unresolved anger and hostility continue to surface in myriad and usually destructive ways.

The process of true forgiveness consists of a number of steps that eventually lead to the freedom forgiveness brings.

### Table 8.3
## A Process of Forgiveness

1. Acknowledge the hurt and affirm the pain. Admitting the hurt is often difficult, but it is a necessary beginning point.
2. Make a decision to forgive. This is an act of the will and may be contrary to the feelings that flow from the hurt. At the beginning you may not know how you will forgive, but you know that you desire to forgive.
3. Remember that forgiveness is a process. Hurt, whether physical or psychological, takes time to heal. Be patient with yourself.
4. Forgiveness involves a "small death" to ourselves. It is not easy, nor is it pleasant.
5. Reflect on those who have modeled forgiveness for you. Can you identify the source of their courage to forgive?
6. Forgive yourself. Separate yourself from your offensive behavior. Try to see the good in yourself even as you disapprove the behavior.
7. Visualize the positive aspects of the person who has offended you. Attempt to understand the cause of the behavior of the other. Try to experience pity or compassion for them.
8. Recall a time in your life when you were forgiven and the gratitude you experienced. Recall how affirming it was to

know someone believed in you and cared enough for you to forgive you.

9. Consider the consequences of not forgiving. Reflect on the short and long-term physiological, spiritual, and emotional effects this will have on you.

10. Ask God's help for the courage to forgive. Do not assume that you will automatically forget, but be patient with yourself and await God's assistance.

11. Celebrate the grace that has empowered you to bring about this Christ-filled moment. Too often we fail to include the element of celebration in the process.

## Effects of Forgiveness

Forgiveness is a choice. To refuse this choice condemns us to a stagnant, unproductive personal and communal life, obsessed with the hurts of the past. One of the most difficult challenges of the spiritual journey is to love ourselves as we have been loved. It involves loving every aspect of self, the shadow side, the weaknesses, the brokenness, everything that is a part of who we are. The temptation is to ignore or hide these parts. Instead, the challenge is to embrace our limitations, to realize that we are being invited to love ourselves as God loves us—the gifted, the wounded, the blessed, and the broken aspects of our beings. We are invited to forgive ourselves for all that we find unacceptable and wearisome in ourselves, and to allow God to work in us. When we realize how much God has forgiven us, we can be more forgiving of others. The cost of that forgiveness has already been paid in the love of Christ on the cross.

## Summary

Genuine forgiveness is not easily cultivated, especially where we have been deeply wounded by another person and our human dignity has been affronted. Forgiveness is no simple feat. To begin, we need to confront and affirm our anger, our pain, and our sense of betrayal. Ultimately, though, it is the act of choosing to forgive that allows us to enjoy the present.

## Suggested Readings

Augsburger, David. *Caring Enough to Forgive*. Scottdale, PA: Herald Press, 1961, pp. 84-140.

Hinnebusch, Paul, O.P. *Community in the Lord*. Notre Dame, IN: Ave Maria Press, 1975, Part V, pp. 139-166.

"I Spoke as a Brother: A Pardon from the Pontiff, A Lesson in Forgiveness for a Troubled World," *Time*, January 9, 1884. *National Catholic Reporter*. Dec. 6, 1996 (Cardinal Bernardin).

Shea, John. *The Challenge of Jesus*. Chicago, IL: Thomas More Press, 1975, chapter 6.

Sofield, Loughlan, Carroll Juliano, and Rosine Hammett. *Design for Wholeness*. Notre Dame, IN: Ave Maria Press, 1990, chapter 3.

## Reflection Questions

1. Remember a time when you have been hurt by someone close to you. What do you remember about the experience and its impact on you? Were there times long after the situation was resolved that hurt feelings surfaced again? How did you deal with these feelings?
2. What have you learned from your experience of interacting with people who have been hurt?
3. Are there people in my community whom I have failed to forgive? What prevents me from forgiving those who have offended me?
4. Who are my models for forgiveness?
5. Can I recall any instances when I offered or received forgiveness? What difference did it make?

## Process for Group Sharing

1. Invite each member to discuss the insights gleaned from completing Worksheet 8.A.
2. Ask a couple of members in advance to prepare a reconciliation service for the community.

## Worksheet 8.A
# Personal Reflections on Forgiveness

People Who Have Modeled Forgiveness for Me

1.

2.

3.

My Reasons for Forgiving

1.

2.

3.

My Personal Obstacles to Forgiveness

1.

2.

3.

# 9

# *Community for Mission*

*Get up and walk.*
*—Luke 5:23*

A leader of a Christian community paraphrased the above quote from the gospel of Saint Luke as the theme of her "state of the union" message to the community. She declared with great passion, "Get up and move!" Though the articulated purpose of the group was apostolic, the leader was increasingly concerned about a phenomenon of "nesting" that she was observing within the community. It appeared that many members evidenced a greater concern for their own comfort than for mission. For them, community had become a comfortable, safe haven. They had become content with a life of prayer and dialogue, but there was a dearth of apostolic action. The community was in process of becoming more sedentary than peripatetic. The leader did not question that their prayer was efficacious or that their dialogue was honest. Rather, she reminded them that as a self-proclaimed apostolic Christian community, they were called beyond prayer and discussion. They were called to service, to be an apostolic, generative community.

Bishop Crispian Hollis, in his opening address to the Joint Council of Priests and Laity of the Diocese of Portsmouth (England), stated his expectation for that council. His comments provide an apt "warning" for any community:

> I issue just one warning and it is this: this Council must not be simply a talking shop, but a representative gathering of disciples with a common aim, and a common mission, and overwhelming determination and commitment to evangelization.[1]

Bishop Hollis' dynamic description closely parallels Avery Dulles' depiction of the church as a "community of disciples"[2] as he stresses the intimate connection between community and discipleship. Bishop Hollis places emphasis on three related, active elements: discipleship, mission, and evangelization. He offers clear criteria for any community that describes itself as Christian:

1. To what extent are the members of the community committed to discipleship?
2. Is the goal of the community mission-centered?
3. Does membership in this community compel its members to become active evangelizers, committed to proclaiming the gospel?

By its very nature, Christian community is apostolic; it never exists solely for its own sake. The local church is called to embody the driving force of communion and mission.

> Communion and mission are profoundly connected with each other; they interpenetrate and mutually imply each other, to the point that communion represents both the source and the fruit of mission. . . . It is always one and the same Spirit who calls together and unifies the Church and sends her to preach the gospel to the ends of the earth *(Christifidelis Laici #32).*[3]

The community is the milieu where the individual Christian is nurtured, supported, and challenged to live the fullness of the Christian vocation. According to the National Conference of Catholic Bishops, that Christian vocation encompasses four elements: each Christian is called to holiness, community, ministry/mission, and Christian maturity. The community exists to facilitate every aspect of that call, including ministry and mission. Yet there comes a time in the life of every community when there is a tendency toward nesting, valuing affiliation, relationships, and closeness more than ministry and mission.

> Basic Christian communities . . . must always be characterized by a decisive universal and missionary thrust that instills in them a renewed apostolic dynamism *(Octogensima Adveniens #25).*[4]

Michael Cowan and Bernard Lee have undertaken a major study of small Christian communities. They are unambiguous in declaring that communities will either cease to function or become ineffectual unless they continue to develop an element of mission.

> Small Christian communities in this country will be a blip on the screen of ecclesial history, rather than an engaging, strong narrative if communities do not have proactive conversation with the world beyond their community membership, as well as effective mutual conversation with each other.[5]

The above statements do not imply that every Christian community is called to engage in a corporate apostolate. Rather, every member of a Christian community, as a result of that membership, should come both to an awareness of this call to ministry and to a discernment of where God is calling him or her to engage in ministry. For most people, the call to ministry is found in the daily circumstances of their lives, their homes, neighborhoods, and workplaces. Some are called to ministry and service within the institutional church.

When a community begins to focus predominately on itself and neglects its apostolic emphasis, it jeopardizes the right to be called Christian. At a recent symposium, Archbishop Thomas Kelly, the Ordinary of the Archdiocese of Louisville, stated, "As a reflection of church community, the community is not a unit closed in upon itself." Avery Dulles, the Jesuit theologian, cautioned against this same temptation when he described his fear that the church, the ultimate Christian community, might become too "ecclesiocentric."

> The Church has become too introverted. . . . Its activities are primarily directed toward the institution and pastoral care of its own members, whose needs and demands tax the institution to its limits.[6]

Peter Drucker, a business management specialist, in an article in *Christian Century* (October 3, 1994) states, "Any enterprise begins to die when it's run for the benefit of the insider rather than for the benefit of outsiders."

Some community members seem to embrace the words the impetuous Saint Peter uttered after witnessing the dazzling transfiguration, "Lord, how good that we are here! With your permission, I will erect three booths here, one for you, one for Moses, and one for Elijah" (Mt 17:4). Peter was prepared to nest. However, Jesus' words to him are the words those who desire to stay put must also hear, "Get up! Do not be afraid" (Mt 17:7).

There is a point in the life of every community when the temptation to opt for security over prophecy, affiliation over mission, and peace over conflict and confrontation is strongest. This usually occurs during the stage of cohesion, shortly after the community has passed successfully through the difficult stage of conflict and is experiencing a period of relative peace and unity. Leaders have the responsibility to challenge communities when they are tempted to settle into this comfort zone. Leaders must remind their members of the reason for creating community in the first place: to serve others. Leadership bears the responsibility continually to goad the community with the challenge, "Get up and move!"

David Nygren and Miriam Ukeritis in their FORUS study discovered that in religious congregations, "affiliation is generally stronger than vision." A report on their study in *America* (September 26, 1992) discussed some implications of what they refer to as "affiliative decline," that is, a greater commitment to belonging than to mission. Nygren and Ukeritis believe that "congregations will decline if members have no stronger reason to remain than mere bonding." This reaffirms the insight of Drucker that organizations begin the process of dying when their focus is more internal than external. Nygren and Ukeritis' predictions apply to religious congregations as well as to any community that seeks to be a Christian community. The decision to move from the comfort of the cohesive, nesting community to an apostolic one is usually met with rather intense resistance on the part of many members. Effective, confrontative leaders attempting to challenge the community beyond its need for safety and security are guaranteed to experience hostile, impassioned resistance, which at times can be intense.

We witnessed a community that was engaged in making a difficult, potentially divisive, and conflictual apostolic decision. The group appeared to be at the cohesive stage of community, the period when there is relative peace and satisfaction within the community. Recently this community had dealt forthrightly, honestly, and courageously with some difficult, conflictual issues that had paralyzed the group for a long period. Now, there was a struggle evident in the minds and hearts of the members. Intellectually, they knew they existed for apostolic purposes. Emotionally, they felt pulled to savor the recently acquired peace and sense of unity, affiliation, safety, and security. Ultimately, they chose affiliation over mission. This is not an unusual decision. At times of high cohesion and affiliation, there is a tendency in many groups to flee to "group think," an unconscious collusion to avoid making the obvious but difficult gospel decisions. Instead their decisions reinforced the pleasant and reassuring feelings of safety and security. This particular community had engaged in a protracted and heated discussion. At the conclusion of the discussion, a vote was taken and the results showed seventeen members in favor of the proposal and two opposed. At that point, someone speaking with great emotion reminded the community that if they were to make this decision based on the vote, they might alienate the two members who were opposed and possibly destroy the unity and cohesion that had taken so long to develop. A second vote was called for, and without any further discussion, the group voted sixteen to three against the same proposal that they had just overwhelmingly approved! Their conviction, perhaps unconscious, was that it was more important to maintain unity than to make the best gospel decision. This group is not unique. We have seen similar dynamics with a number of other groups with whom we have worked.

On February 22, 1989, Pope John Paul II sent a letter to the bishops of the United States in response to the report of the pontifical commission established to study religious life in the United States. Although the focus of the study and the pope's comments were directed toward religious congregations in the United States, his words are appropriate for all communities: "Community life is intended to be life-giving." He goes on to state clearly that he does not "advocate a closed, static, merely formalistic" community, but rather "a healthy and vibrant" one. Healthy and vibrant communities are apostolic. Closed, static, formalistic communities become nesting communities. The pope also voiced apprehension that there might be more concern about the needs of members than the needs of the people they are sent to serve. In essence, he offers the challenge to resist the attraction toward the greatest enemy of community, narcissism.

The concern voiced by the pope may reflect a growing phenomenon, especially in the United States, if what is reported by social scientists is accurate. Wade Clark Roof, who has done major research on the baby boomers, "the generation of seekers," says that they "turn to small groups and lifestyle enclaves in search of a quality of belonging." He also hypothesizes that boomers in these settings look for "sharing, caring, accepting, and belonging." While these qualities can be positive, if they become the major focus of self-proclaimed apostolic communities, they can be destructive. The challenge for all communities is to develop these positive qualities without making them the end-product of the community.

We had the opportunity to work with a dynamic apostolic, generative parish community that has resisted the pull toward the narcissism of the baby boomers. It is a vital community that years ago made a decision for mission rather than maintenance. They chose as their mission statement a simple but profound four word dictum, "To Feed the Poor." All monies earned in parish fund-raising activities, approximately a quarter of a million dollars a year, are used to feed the poor. Not one penny raised through fund-raising activities is used for the internal needs of the parish. The money is spent to meet the immediate needs of the poor but is also disbursed to third world countries for projects to assure that starving people can initiate new ventures to feed themselves.

This parish is an example of what is often described as a "magnet parish." People travel great distances to be members of this worshipping, apostolic community. Parishioners often cross parish geographic boundaries to worship with this community. What is most evident to a visitor is the dynamism of the parishioners. Life-filled and life-giving communities attract dynamic people. Non-apostolic, self-serving parishes attract people who are more concerned about meeting their own needs than about serving others. We encounter many church organizations and Christian communities that have developed beautifully articulated, long, descriptive "mission statements." However, these statements often have little to do with mission. To call them mission statements is a misnomer. They are usually carefully crafted documents that help to make a community feel proud of itself. What is your stated mission statement? Is it truly apostolic and missionary in scope?

The National Conference of Catholic Bishops has recently published a document on young adult ministry, *Sons and Daughters of the Light*, which clearly identifies the purpose of community to be missionary. Although they direct their challenge to parish and campus communities, it is really a universal challenge to every Christian community.

The mission of the parish or campus community is not directed solely at itself but at nurturing and forming people to be leaven in society.[7]

The ultimate challenge for every Christian community is to evaluate itself against the criterion that characteristically makes it Christian, that is, whether its primary focus is apostolic, external to the community. This is a challenge, especially in light of the prevailing attitudes of the society in which we live, which runs counter to this focus. Christian communities are clearly called to be countercultural.

## Summary

Christian community by definition is an apostolic community. Christian community never exists solely for its own sake but, primarily, to foster the mission of Jesus Christ. In the life of every community, there comes a time when the community must choose between the pull toward merely focusing on the need to belong and the countervailing force, a need to be generative, to be apostolic. This option for mission demands strong and secure leadership willing to challenge continually the complacency of the community, even in the midst of forceful resistance.

## Suggested Readings

Dulles, Avery, "John Paul II and the New Evangelization," *America*, February 1, 1992, Vol. 166, #3, pp. 52-72.

Foundations and Donors Interested in Catholic Activities, Inc. *Future of Religious Life: Implications for Religious Identity, Leadership and Vocations: Proceedings of a National Symposium*. Washington, DC: FADICA, 1993.

National Conference of Catholic Bishops. *Called and Gifted for the Third Millennium: Reflections of the U.S. Catholic Bishops on the Thirtieth Anniversary of the Decree on the Apostolate of the Laity and the Fifteenth Anniversary of Called and Gifted*. Washington, DC: NCCB/USCC, 1995.

Nygren, David and Miriam Ukeritis, "Future of Religious Orders in the United States," *Origins*, Vol. 22: No. 15, September 24, 1992, pp. 257-272.

Roof, Wade Clark. *A Generation of Seekers: The Spiritual Journeys of the Baby Boom Generation*. San Francisco: HarperSan Francisco, chapter 9.

# Reflection Questions

1. Have I observed times in this community when there was a tendency to nest, to choose affiliation over mission? Why did this occur and how did we respond?
2. What militates against committing ourselves to a greater sense of mission?
3. How do we empower our leadership to call us beyond complacency, safety, and security?
4. What is our mission statement? How truly missionary is it?

# Process for Group Sharing

1. Identify and address the ways in which your group might tend to be more affiliative than mission-oriented. Be as specific and honest as possible.
2. Determine what steps to take in order to maintain a mission focus.
3. Reaffirm a commitment to leadership, empowering them to continue to call the community to a mission-orientation.

·

# 10

# Communal Decision-Making: Appropriate and Effective?

*They then drew lots for them, and as the lot fell to Matthias, he was listed as one of the twelve apostles.*

—*Acts 1:26*

The issue of decision-making has been hotly debated in recent years. There are some individuals and communities that have seemed to canonize certain forms of decision-making while completely negating other methods. It is our belief that no one decision-making method is applicable in all situations. Instead, we suggest that two criteria should be applied: first, what is the most appropriate method to use in this particular case; and second, which method will be most effective in helping to achieve one's goals. These two criteria, appropriateness and effectiveness, should be the primary yardsticks in determining which form of decision-making to employ in any given situation.

We are indebted to Father William Burkert, S.T., for the development of Table 10.1. He identifies a number of distinct methods for decision-making, highlighting both the advantages and disadvantages of each method. Burkert proposes that a community discuss each of the options, asking, "From your experience, where has this method been effective and appropriate?" This exercise sensitizes the community to applying the two criteria of effectiveness and appropriateness. Burkert relates effectiveness with the ability to accomplish a task and appropriateness with the suitability of the approach. For example, if one member fell and broke a leg, it would be most effective and appropriate for someone to make a unilateral decision to get proper medical care as quickly as possible for that person. Obviously, any method involving discussion, voting, or consensus would be ineffective and inappropriate.

We have developed Burkert's model for use in this book.

**Table 10.1**

# Decision-Making Methods

### 1. Authority Rule Without Discussion

**Example:** Leader informs community of a decision he or she has made.

**Disadvantages:** Decision dependent on the wisdom of a single person; advantages of group interactions and wisdom is lost; may discourage any commitment to implementing the decision on the part of other members; possible resentment may result in sabotage of any progress.

**Advantages:** Especially useful for simple, routine decisions; effective when very little time is available to make the decision, when group members expect the designated leader to make the decision, and when there is a lack of skills and information among group members to make the decision in an appropriate manner.

### 2. Delegation to Expert

**Example:** Identify and delegate someone with a certain expertise to make the decision.

**Disadvantages:** It may be difficult to determine who the expert is, especially if members are not aware of each other's gifts; ownership of the decision and commitment to implementation may be minimal; advantage of group interaction is lost; minimal use of the resources of other members.

**Advantages:** Useful when the expertise of one person is so far superior to that of all other group members that little is to be gained by discussion; should be used when the need for membership action in implementing the decision is slight; affirms the unique expertise and gifts of members.

### 3. Sampling of Members' Opinions

**Example:** Leader takes a general pulse of the community and decides.

**Disadvantages:** There is not enough interaction among group members for them to gain from each other's resources and to get the benefits of group discussion; unresolved conflict and controversy may emerge in indirect ways, damaging future group effectiveness.

**Advantages:** Useful in a situation where it is difficult to get group members to talk, when the decision is so urgent that there is no time for group discussion, when member commitment is not necessary for implementing the decision, and when a lack of skills and information exists among group members so that it is important to make the decision any other way.

## 4. Authority Rule After Discussion

**Example:** Leader consults with group and makes decision after discussion.

**Disadvantages:** Could develop minimal commitment for implementing the decision; does not resolve the controversies and conflicts among group members; tends to create situations in which group members either compete to impress the designated leader or tell the leader what they think he or she wants to hear; often results in decreased sense of self-esteem among members.

**Advantages:** Involves the membership and uses their resources more fully than the previous methods; gains some of the benefits of group discussion; involves consultation when the leader has the responsibility to make a difficult decision.

## 5. Majority Control

**Example:** Community takes vote.

**Disadvantages:** May leave an alienated minority; could result in a sense of winners and losers; commitment for implementing the decision may be diminished.

**Advantages:** Will usually result in a commitment of the majority of members; appropriate and effective when there is a decision by the membership that the issue should not consume a disproportionate amount of time or energy; brings closure to issues that are difficult to resolve.

## 6. Minority Control

**Example:** A small committee is authorized to make the decision.

**Disadvantages:** Does not utilize the resources of many group members; does not establish widespread commitment to the decision; not much benefit from group interaction; leaves the majority often feeling used or devalued.

**Advantages:** Can be used when everyone cannot meet to make a decision, when the group is under such time pressure that it must delegate responsibility to a committee, when only a few members have any relevant resources, or when broad member commitment is not needed to implement the decision.

## 7. Consensus

**Example:** All community members involved in and agree to the decision.

**Disadvantages:** Takes a great deal of time and psychological energy and a high level of member skill; may arrive at least common denominator; sometimes opts for cohesion over gospel-oriented decisions; can prolong decision around issues that are urgent.

**Advantages:** Can increase the level of commitment by all members; uses the resources of all members; provides a process to deal with difficult decisions that affect all.

**8. Discernment**

**Example:** A prayerful process of weighing the pros and cons of the decision is engaged in before the community comes to a decision.

**Disadvantages:** Is a very time-consuming process; can become a very burdensome process for decisions that can be made more simply; requires a high level of maturity and freedom on the part of all members.

**Advantages:** Provides a prayerful process for deciding; encourages each member to look at a situation both positively and negatively; often gains the greatest commitment to decision reached.

We invite you to complete Worksheets 10.A and 10.B. Worksheet 10.A asks you to identify your own beliefs about the advantages and disadvantages of each decision-making process. If you wish, add additional decision-making processes not included in this list. Worksheet 10.B asks you to identify specific situations in which you might use each of these processes.

## Consensual Decision-Making

From our experience of working with communities, we raise a word of caution. For some communities, consensus as a method of decision-making is held up as the ideal with all other decision-making processes relegated to a secondary, and at times, merely tolerated, status.

Consensus is a valid, appropriate, and effective method for decision-making in some situations, but not all. To utilize consensus in all decision-making situations weakens its continued effectiveness and may, on occasion, drain necessary energy away from the apostolic pursuits of the community or lead to communal gridlock.

## The Case for Consensus

Consensus is most valid when the decision includes these elements: the decision is a major one; it affects the long-range pastoral mission; it has serious implications for the majority of people within the community; and, no simpler, equally effective, and appropriate method would achieve the same results.

While there are many different understandings of consensus, the following seems to be a good working definition: Consensus is a process of decision-making in which the whole community agrees to a common course of action that preserves the values of all and is eventually owned by all.

The purpose of this chapter is not to denigrate consensus, but to raise some questions that will help communities utilize the process in a more selective way.

112

# Some Concerns About Consensus

Consensus has certainly been used in ways that have enhanced the life of the members and of the communities. However, we have also observed times when consensus has been misused. These experiences led us to review leadership material being generated referring to the use of consensus. This material provides data that raise some significant questions and concerns about consensus.

## Our Experience

The primary emphasis of our ministry focuses on assisting groups to develop a greater quality of communal life and to minister more collaboratively.

As described in chapter 1, our approach is predicated on a developmental model of community that focuses on predictable stages through which each group progresses. In the earlier developmental stages, consensus may be effective and appropriate. Once a group has faced and successfully addressed conflict, it enters the stage of cohesion, which is characterized by a rather comfortable and pleasant sense of unity and relative peace. In our experience, this stage of cohesion, as was mentioned in Section I, is the least effective time to employ consensus. Having finally achieved some relative state of unity, the group is reluctant to engage in any behavior that might threaten or disrupt this tenuous feeling of cohesion and unity. Unconsciously, the group often opts for a decision that will retain the pleasant, secure atmosphere. Without realizing it, the group may elect for decision-making criteria that will maintain the peace, rather than opt for a decision which will be mission-oriented and helpful in accomplishing the mission. "Peace at any price" becomes more than just a clever cliché; it becomes the norm. Also, during the cohesive stage there is a tendency for the group to nest and to bask in their achieved unity and peace. The group has to be reminded that Christian communities always exist for the sake of mission, not just so that members will enjoy the warmth and security of community. Groups who engage in consensus at this time will often drift toward decisions whose primary end is to avoid alienating any group member.

Thus, without realizing it, the group may choose survival or maintenance over mission because of their desire to keep a unified status quo. The health of the group is at stake. A reminder from the World Health Organization may be in order: health goes beyond merely the absence of disease and includes the ability to thrive, not merely survive.

Jesus was a radical prophetic figure. He stirred the overly-comfortable and challenged the status quo. Likewise, Christianity is a prophetic religion distinguished by its willingness to confront and challenge what is not gospel. This is true even when the confrontation may "rock the boat" and produce tension and alienation.

We have encountered some groups who are convinced that consensus is the most "gospel" form of decision-making. However,

113

this belief is not substantiated in scripture. There is no evidence of a time or situation in the early church where consensus was used as a decision-making method. There is ample reference to other methods, even including the drawing of lots.

Though our concerns about consensus come from our own experience, recent studies on effective communities are voicing similar concerns.

## FORUS Study

David Nygren and Miriam Ukeritis have undertaken a substantial study on the transformation and future of religious life in the United States. Their research unearthed valuable data, not only for religious congregations, but for all Christian communities. Among the areas explored was the issue of decision-making as related to leadership. Their study makes valuable distinctions between male and female leadership, and typical and outstanding leaders.

Nygren and Ukeritis state that consensual decision-making "builds high affiliation but low instrumentality." Groups that rely exclusively on consensus as the major or only form of decision-making may develop good interpersonal relationships and nurture a cohesive climate, but these groups may not be effective in making decisions which will foster the mission of the organization.

Nygren and Ukeritis raise several areas for consideration. Pointing to the current confusion over authority and leadership, they identify two concepts that contribute to this confusion: "team leadership" and "consensual decision-making." While both of these concepts can be potentially effective, Nygren and Ukeritis express some level of concern. Team leadership and consensual decision-making can have a paralyzing effect on the visionary leader, as well as result in "mediocre management, representing the least common denominator within an organization." They also caution that "variable understandings of consensus" can confuse the ultimate ability of the group to allow those in leadership to function effectively.

A myth has developed during the last two decades, i.e., that the most mature groups are those who do not have designated leaders and who make all decisions by consensus. On the contrary, research and study on groups indicates that leaderless groups are not mission-effective. Refusing to give one person or small group authority to make decisions and opting only for a consensual form of decision-making may indeed be an immature approach. Perhaps the question can be asked, "Are we mature enough to allow a member or members to utilize their gift of leadership?"

Letty Russell cautions against the simplistic solution that eliminates all authority and leadership:

> Some argue that we must do away with all hierarchy and leadership in order to be truly partners. This doesn't take into account the fact that human organization always involve power dynamics, and that these are likely to be more destructive when they are not recognized and channeled constructively towards a common goal.[1]

## Spirit-linking Leadership

In an informative and provocative article in *Human Development*, Donna Markham describes a model of leadership that she defines as spirit-linking leadership. Within this article she develops the theme of consensus further, indicating that consensual decision-making may lead to the development of decisions which lack a personal, passionate commitment. Markham summarizes her belief by declaring, "consensus . . . often resulted in decisions that no one really felt passionate about—and without passion, excitement, and energy, there is no commitment."

According to Markham, one reason why consensus may be overvalued is that it may be the unconscious choice of people who fear conflict. The National Conference of Catholic Bishops conducted two research projects: one on priests and another on the non-ordained working in the parish. The projects show that both these groups have difficulty dealing with conflict. Not only is conflict avoided, but the emotions surrounding conflict when it does occur are not acceptable. Individuals fearful and paralyzed by conflict may invoke consensual decision-making as a panacea.

Markham hypothesizes that much of the *ennui* which exists in our Christian institutions may be traced to the consensual decisions which have determined future directions in those institutions. Consensus may result in decisions that do not galvanize the energy to implement what has been decided. Markham concludes:

> The problem was that no one believed deeply that the decision should be carried out, so no one felt compelled to alter the status quo. Today we must move beyond consensus, which has often led to mediocrity.

This premise was confirmed for us in a recent discussion we had with people in leadership of Christian communities. They stated that it is easier to get people excited and committed to projects which they personally have initiated rather than to projects which are the result of consensual decisions.

## Edwin Friedman

Edwin Friedman was a noted and reputable systems therapist who consulted with a variety of organizations and institutions. One of his fundamental premises was that "Consensus, while still an important goal, is not to be confused with a way of life."

Friedman identified the two least effective methods of decision-making as charismatic leadership and consensus. While each model has positive elements, it can also be potentially harmful or destructive. For instance, Friedman notes:

> The charismatic personality can unify disparate elements, inspire contagious enthusiasm, and galvanize a family into quick action. It seems to work best when the relationship system is despondent, helpless, confused, and hungry for change. Demagogy, whether it is political, religious, or therapeutic is always most attractive in a depression.

115

Friedman likewise shows both the advantages and disadvantages of consensus:

> In the consensus approach . . . the group is prepared to wait longer for results, being more concerned with the development of a cohesive infrastructure. It tends to value peace over progress and personal relationships, or feelings over ideas. In such a setting, undue individualism of a leader is more likely to create anxiety than reduce it.

Friedman identifies a number of potential difficulties with consensus leadership. A primary difficulty is that the group will tend to be less imaginative. He is convinced that the world's most important ideas come to people in solitude. He believes that the consensus approach discourages idiosyncrasy and originality. As stated earlier, leaderless groups are more prone to anxiety, an anxiety that can tend, in Friedman's words, to "cascade." Perhaps the most negative aspect of consensus identified by Friedman is one to which religiously-oriented groups, especially those struggling with cohesion, can fall victim. Emphasis on consensus gives strength to the extremists because they can continue to dangle the carrot of unity as their price for cooperation. Friedman hypothesizes that consensus ultimately may create the very polarization it attempts to avoid:

> Ironically, as a consensus-based approach to leadership nears its goal, the degree of emotional fusion that results is likely to create the very problems its approach was designed to avoid.

## Liberum Veto

In the book *Poland*, James Michener comments on an aspect of the government in ancient Poland called *liberum veto*. This allowed one man in the parliament of hundreds to negate the entire work of that assembly by merely crying, "I oppose!" Michener believes that this was a major cause of Poland's disappearance from the map of Europe. One can easily see the connection between this and what often occurs with consensual decision-making in church groups today. When one person claims that he or she cannot live with the consequences of a decision, the group grants absolute power to the dissenter, thus preventing the movement of the group. In reality, adopting a model of decision-making that allows a single individual to prevent decisions because of his or her inability to "live" with the decision grants the ultimate decision-making power to a single individual or a small group. The minority, even a minority of one, ultimately controls the decision. In some groups, especially those with dysfunctional members, this individual or minority can hold the group "hostage" if consensus is taken too literally. Many religiously-oriented people seem to eschew voting for fear of the effect on the minority. This view fails to see that the group may be potentially granting absolute authority to a minority of one.

# Accountability

There are three major reasons why communities fail. First, a mutual, common purpose is absent. Second, too many members do not possess the capacity, ability, or maturity to achieve the common purpose. Third, the community has failed to develop appropriate and effective structures and processes for accountability.

The third reason relates directly to decision-making. While communities are willing to expend time and energy in determining which method of decision-making to employ, they may neglect provision for establishing adequate structures for accountability. In your community, what processes and structures assure that a decision is implemented? In what ways do members hold each other accountable for what has been mutually agreed upon?

When adequate methods for accountability are not part of the decision-making process, failure and frustration are sure to result.

# Summary

Consensus is a valid, appropriate, and effective form of decision-making when used judiciously and applied reasonably. However, it is only one of many valid, appropriate, and effective methods. The overuse or misuse of consensus can have serious repercussions on the growth and mission of the Christian community.

A number of reputable social scientists raise legitimate questions and concerns about consensus. Failure to consider these concerns can condemn a community to stagnation and *ennui*, and perhaps threaten its very survival.

# Suggested Readings

Foundations and Donors Interested in Catholic Activities. *The Future of Religious Life: Implications for Religious Identity, Leadership and Vocations*. 1993.

Friedman, Edwin H. "Emotional Process in the Marketplace: The Family Therapist as Consultant with Work Systems" in McDaniel, Susan, Lyman Wynn, and Timothy Weber, *Systems Consultation: A New Perspective for Families*. New York: Guilford, 1986.

Markham, Donna, "Spiritlinking Leadership," *Human Development*, Vol. 15, #3, Fall 1994.

Nygren, David and Miriam Ukeritis, "Research Executive Summary: Future of Religious Orders in the United States,"*Origins*, September 24, 1992, Vol. 22: No. 15.

## Reflection Questions

1. How do we apply the criteria of appropriateness and effectiveness in making decisions in our community?
2. Am I willing to consider the validity of decision-making methods other than consensus?
3. If I apply the criteria of effectiveness and appropriateness to the last three decisions we made as a community, what method of decision-making would I now choose in each of those situations?

## Process for Group Sharing

1. Review your responses to Worksheet 10.B.
2. Have the members share their insights as a result of engaging in this exercise.
3. Identify a number of issues that the group must address in the immediate future and discuss which decision-making option seems most effective and appropriate (see Worksheet 10.C).
4. If time allows, invite each member to share his or her own beliefs about consensual decision-making.

# Worksheet 10.A

| Decision-Making Process | Disadvantages | Advantages |
| --- | --- | --- |
| 1. Authority Rule Without Discussion | | |
| 2. Delegation to Expert | | |
| 3. Sampling of Members' Opinions | | |
| 4. Authority Rule After Discussion | | |
| 5. Majority Control | | |
| 6. Minority Control | | |
| 7. Consensus | | |
| 8. Discernment | | |
| 9. _____ | | |
| 10. _____ | | |

# Worksheet 10.B

| Decision-Making Process | Situation Where It Would Be Appropriate and Effective |
|---|---|
| 1. Authority Rule Without Discussion | |
| 2. Delegation to Expert | |
| 3. Sampling of Members' Opinions | |
| 4. Authority Rule After Discussion | |
| 5. Majority Control | |
| 6. Minority Control | |
| 7. Consensus | |
| 8. Discernment | |

## Worksheet 10.C
# Pending Decisions

| Issues to Be Decided | Suggested Decision-Making Method to Be Used | Reasons for Suggesting This Method |
|---|---|---|
| | | |

# 11
# Faith-Sharing

*"Stand up and go on your way. Your*
*faith has saved you."*
*—Luke 17:19*

Faith-sharing is the shared reflection of the community's common experience of God—how God continually touches each individual and how, in turn, each responds to that touch. Faith-sharing is an act of absolute trust. It willingly invites others into the sacred space of one's inner world of beliefs, values, commitments, doubts, and difficulties. As community members listen to one another's story and experience, an appreciation grows of how God is at work in each one's life. The purpose of faith-sharing is to hear the ever new word and will of God as it is revealed to the Christian community through each individual faith story.

Faith-sharing is a verbal present-day repetition of what the evangelists did when they wrote the gospels and what the prophets did through their lives and words. It is a sharing of the good news. It is the revelation of God's presence as it comes to life through the sharing of God's people. The "kingdom of God" is not long ago or somewhere in the future. The kingdom of God is now—"for behold, the kingdom of God is in your midst" (Lk 17:20). The act of sharing faith in communities makes the kingdom present in the community. Through faith-sharing, we become more aware of our call to participate in fostering the kingdom and receive the strength and encouragement do so.

Faith-sharing calls us to share with each other what it means to be a follower of Christ in the world today. Through authentic faith-sharing, we come to know and love the others in Christ whose Spirit is the bonding force of community.

A faith-sharing group is not a discussion group; neither is it a sensitivity session or a social gathering. The purpose of faith-sharing is to experience the presence of God incarnate within the Christian community. The fruit of faith-sharing is the building up of the Christian community (Eph 4:12).

## Why Faith-Sharing Is Important

Sharing faith in community affords many graces both to the individual and the community.

### Table 11.1
### Benefits of Faith-Sharing

- Reveals one's personal role in salvation history
- Deepens relation with God
- Helps to discover one's true self
- Heals loneliness and brokenness
- Provides a new perception of life
- Ultimately, fosters the development of community

Faith-sharing takes people out of the realm of ideas into the realm of experience. It opens them to the realization that their experiences are valid and good. It eliminates the need to justify those experiences. Participating in faith-sharing allows the members to see their lives as a "salvation history." They acknowledge and appreciate more fully God's presence in the seemingly ordinary events of daily life. The recounting of faith stories helps to make God's plan more apparent. It highlights the relationship and responsibility that each has in the divine plan of extending the kingdom.

This recounting in prayer of the elements of daily life reveals the sometimes obscure presence of the Redeemer in one's spiritual journey. It often provides greater clarity about one's personal call. Faith-sharing provides an opportunity to deepen one's relationship with God through sharing of prayer, of faith, and of God's action in the daily circumstances of life. As a group listens to God disclosed through these sharings, the Lord is introduced anew to each individual.

Christian life is a spiritual journey—a journey into God, a journey into one's true self. In discovering and owning one's true self through the process of sharing faith, there is a rediscovery of God—the root and ground of all being. Life's journey is not a solitary venture. Each person is born into a community. Community and human solidarity are what human life is all about. God reveals the fullness of divine love first in community, especially through the mutual sharing of faith.

In addition to helping the community experience God's presence, faith-sharing is also a powerful source of healing. It assuages and removes the anguish of loneliness. The sharing of each member's personal experiences corroborates the crucial attachment of all as daughters and sons of a loving God. There is a sense of oneness, unity, and connectedness. Faith-sharing removes the barriers that divide and grants permission to enter into that sacred place within every person where "spirit touches spirit." In the sharing of this deeply personal and mysterious aspect of oneself, there is the profound discovery of experiences, questions, and concerns that are shared by each. To enter authentically into faith-sharing is to come to know and love each other in Christ.

Sharing faith opens a whole new way of looking at life as new perceptions emerge. People see the Lord working in ways never thought possible as they see their lives as an integral part of salvation history.

Through faith-sharing, a community is created and relationships deepen as individuals grow. Alone each person never achieves his or her highest ideals, but when united with others in heart and in action, wondrous things occur. For each person there is a growing awareness of God's salvific activity. This awareness is strengthened and made manifest by the witness of others' sharing. Through this sharing, they discover more fully how God is at work even when there is little conscious awareness of the divine presence. The sharing also witnesses to the goodness of God and God's action in the world. Sharing of difficulties is especially growth-producing when viewed through the prism of salvation history. It is an enriching awareness merely to think of one's life as "salvation history."

## Beliefs That Facilitate Faith-Sharing

Certain beliefs and attitudes facilitate the sharing of faith. What are your beliefs that either facilitate or impede your willingness to share faith? Compare your beliefs with the ones identified in Table 11.2.

### Table 11.2
## Beliefs That Facilitate Faith-Sharing

- God is revealed and becomes present through my own unique history. Therefore, it is incumbent upon me to spend quality time reflecting on my personal history if I am to discover God in my life. Personal reflection leads to true discernment, to a discovery of where God is leading me. Such reflection is part of what is referred to as "examine of consciousness."

- When I take time to engage in personal reflection, I become aware of the many ways in which God is present to me through the seemingly simple incidents of my life.

- The call to share the good news of God's work in me is a call to accept the fact that I am a special object of God's concern and love. Awareness of this specialness impels me to share the good news with those I encounter.

- Only to the degree that I both freely choose to respond to God's call and grant this same freedom to others will true faith-sharing ensue.

Even in the presence of such positive beliefs, faith-sharing may still be difficult. At best, most people feel ambivalent about risking their most personal experiences of God, very intimate moments, with others. Sometimes the beautiful attitudes present in the list above coexist with other attitudes and beliefs that militate against taking the risk to share at the level of deep faith.

## Table 11.3
# Beliefs That Hinder Faith-Sharing

- It is extremely difficult to identify God's activity in the world.
- I am lacking in humility if I speak of myself as a special object of God's love and concern.
- My faith is a private matter.
- Sharing my relationship with God sometimes means focusing on negative elements in my life which are nobody's business but my own.
- Others will be aware of the inadequacy of my own faith life.
- I cannot trust these people with these sacred experiences.
- The pressure to share in group sessions makes faith-sharing unacceptable.

This final belief regarding the pressure to share requires a response. It is our conviction that communities should foster a climate of freedom, creating that safe, sacred space where people not only feel free to share their faith experiences, but also where they feel free to remain silent. Sometimes the invitation to share faith includes a subtle, or not so subtle, pressure that makes it uncomfortable for people to maintain a sense of silence. This is especially difficult when they are uncomfortable in sharing or when they are not convinced they have anything of value to share. They should under no condition ever be forced to explain or defend their experiences.

Faith-sharing is never to be forced. It happens as each person experiences a growing awareness of God's loving activity and feels drawn to share these experiences with others. Through faith-sharing, a community is created and deepened. As awareness is strengthened by the witness of others, people begin to recognize the Lord's work in their lives in ways they had never before realized. When they do not feel pressured to explain or defend their experiences, a freedom develops. A whole new way of living is opened to them. They become acutely aware of God's presence at every moment of life.

## The Process of Faith-Sharing

There are countless ways to share faith. No one method is sacrosanct. Therefore, in the suggested process section, we provide a variety of methods and forms. Another reason why we offer so many options is that faith-sharing is not something that is done only once. It needs to be repeated often if the community is to grow. It is important that the community feels comfortable with whatever formats are used.

These are not models that are to be followed slavishly, but rather models intended to provide a variety of options.

As persons come together to share, there is a dynamic that builds and allows them to get to know each other at a level different from the usual everyday sharing. The experience is intended to be a religious encounter, a reflection upon the experience of God in one's life—a prayerful experience. There is a sacredness about what is shared, and, frequently, the sharing will not even be followed by discussion or comment. The main benefit lies in the fact that participants simply listen to, accept, and respect each person's experience of God. The simple process of listening to one another, of appreciating the touch of God in each person's life, is truly enriching and life-giving.

## Summary

Any faith community that does not share faith is a contradiction in terms. While the sharing of one's personal faith journey is essential for the growth of the community, it is often a difficult task. It demands a high level of trust for members to share the most sacred and intimate parts of their lives. Many communities experience a great deal of resistance to sharing faith. However, when the sharing is received with the respect and reverence it deserves, the desire and willingness to enter into this form of praying together increases.

Faith-sharing is the coming together of a community, the being present to one another, to remember, to reflect, to share, to give each other the support needed to grow in the awareness of God's presence in the daily events and happenings of life. The more this is done, the more each member is enabled to grow in awareness and acceptance of God's presence everywhere . . . a growing sense that we are *always* in God's presence.

## Suggested Readings

Pable, Martin, OFM Cap., "Models of Faith-Sharing," *Review for Religious*, March-April 1995, pp. 253-260.

Roy, Paul, S.J. *Building Christian Communities for Justice*. New York: Paulist Press, 1981, pp. 74-101 and 150-163.

## Process for Group Sharing

As indicated above, a number of options for sharing are possible. Select the ones that are most appropriate for your community. Invite members to develop other options.

Some of the processes offered were initially developed by Father Jose Esquival, S.J., Father Paul Roy, S.J., and Father John Carroll Futrell, S.J.

### I. Scripture Sharing

1. One person reads a selected scripture passage aloud.
2. Allocate time for quiet reflection on the following:
   a. What word or phrase leaps out at you, and what feeling does it elicit?
   b. What affirmed or encouraged you? What challenged you or made you feel uncomfortable?
   c. What are you going to do to concretize the scripture for yourself?
      What can I *begin* doing?
      What can I *stop* doing?
      What can I *continue* to do better or in a more intentional way? (You have not really heard the gospel if it does not move you to action.)
   d. What can the group do together?
      What can we *begin* doing?
      What can we *stop* doing?
      What can we *continue* to do better or in a more intentional way? (This action must be something concrete that flows out of the reading and reflection.)
3. Invite each member to share responses to one or more of the reflection questions.
4. Challenge each member to listen with faith and openness to the Spirit being revealed.
5. Depending on the interest of the group, group sharing may or may not follow the individual sharing.
6. End with prayer or a song of praise.

## II. The Critical Incident Model
## (reflection on experience)

1. Begin with prayer or scripture reading, e.g., The Lord's Prayer.
2. Select an incident from your past week or two that has stirred up strong emotion.
3. Reflect on questions such as:
   What kind of feelings did the incident stir up in you?
   How did you respond at the time?
   How do you feel about the way you responded?
   What might this response tell you about yourself?
4. Most important, looking back, how can you see God present or active in the incident and in your response?
   What biblical passages or images come to mind?
   What response might God be asking of you now? (praise, gratitude, wonder, repentance, forgiveness, action?)
5. Depending on the interest of the group, group sharing may or may not follow the individual sharing.
6. Conclude with prayer.

## III. Communal Reflection 1

1. Ask members to recall a specific time in their life when they were intently aware of God's presence.
2. Invite them to enter into that experience and encourage them to relive it with all their faculties (emotions, cognition, fantasy, etc.)—luxuriating in the experience once again.
3. Encourage each member to share that experience in any way he or she feels comfortable.
4. Challenge the other members to listen prayerfully and with the ears of faith to the experience being shared.
5. End with a prayer of thanks to God for each of these experiences.

## IV. Communal Reflection 2

1. Reflect on the following:
   Where have I been aware of the presence of God in my life today?
   Where have I specifically experienced God in a person I encountered today?
   Can I identify a particular experience in which I felt drawn closer to God?
   Where did I find God in the silence?
   Where did I experience God in the chaos?

## V. Additional Suggestions for Communal Reflection

1. Genealogy (Mt 13:53-56)

   Who am I? What are the pertinent facts that influence my being, such as my position in the family, my nationality, my first impressions of God, of faith, my personal history?

2. Early Experiences of God (Mt 9:9, Gal 1:11-16)

   What were my early experiences of God?

3. Highlights of God in My Life (Mt 11:1-24)

   What have been my peak experiences of God? What or who speaks to me of God at this time?

4. Who is Jesus for me? What is he in my life? (Mt 16:13-17)

   Where do I find Christ? How does Christ seek me? (This session can be spent in quiet prayer.)

5. The Christ Seal (Mt 7:18)

   Where have I seen God evident in the life of specific individuals in this community? (At this session each person in turn listens as others describe how they see the seal of Christ's action in one another's lives . . . the stamp of Christ's action or gifts. No response is necessary.)

## VI. Gift Sharing

The process for this was described in chapter 6.

# 12
# *Intimacy:*
# *The Heart of Community*

*Jesus wept; and the Jews said, "See how much he loved him!"*
*—John 11:35-36*

Two women were sorting through a collection of watercolor paintings drawn by a friend who had recently died. They admired a number of her paintings as they marked them for distribution to other friends. One unfinished drawing, in particular, caught their attention. It was a lovely house situated on the beach with the ocean in the background. The house was enclosed with a white picket fence. The overall picture was well drawn and attractive, but it had an obvious flaw. The artist had failed in her attempt to construct a realistic-looking fence. The two women looked at each other and thought of their artist friend, a warm-hearted, kind, generous person who gave of herself to so many people. "You know," one woman said to the other, "it shouldn't surprise us that Alice couldn't accurately draw a fence around the house. She didn't know how to draw a fence: she never built any fences in her own life." Alice's unsuccessful attempt to draw a fence represents her personal success in allowing others into her life. It highlights the value of intimacy.

The issue of intimacy pervades the life of any community and is an essential issue for the group to resolve in order to build community. As described in the near/far stage in Section I, discovering a level of intimacy appropriate to the community can present a challenge, for within the assembled community, there are differing expectations with regard to intimacy. In addition, each member possesses different needs and capacities for intimacy. Negotiating an intimacy level at which all members can be comfortable is not achieved quickly or without effort. The successful resolution of this stage of development in the group is dependent on whether the members, like Alice, have acquired some capacity for intimacy in their personal lives.

## Personal Intimacy Defined

Intimacy is one of our basic human needs. In Abraham Maslow's hierarchy of needs, the need for love, affection, belonging to and identifying with others is ranked as one of the higher levels of all human needs.

In addition to being a basic need, intimacy is also a stage of psychosocial development. The study of human development by Eric Erikson[1] teaches that the stage of intimacy first forms in adolescence but continues to undergo development and to be refined as an individual matures. It is at this level of development that an individual can freely enter into partnerships and affiliations and can abide by those commitments. Intimacy is a time when a person can share oneself with another without the fear of losing part of that self in the process. The scope of intimacy encompasses all relationships.

Intimacy is the ability to share oneself with another, to allow another to know some of what self-knowledge has revealed. Self-disclosure calls for a willingness to let an outsider into one's personal space. Openness and freedom are also needed, for intimacy involves risk and leaves a person vulnerable. Security and comfort with one's own identity permits sharing parts of self with another. To establish any level of intimacy in a relationship requires knowledge of that other person over time so that some degree of trust can be built.

## Intimacy and Community

Members bring to community their varying needs and experiences of intimacy. Some members may expect all their intimacy needs to be addressed in community. These unrealistic and unhealthy demands will place pressure on the community, creating a tension that drains the group and detracts from its mission and purpose.

Other members have little or no expectation of intimacy needs in community and therefore stay on the periphery of the group with little personal involvement or interaction with other members. In order to include and involve this type of member, there is need to discuss expectations of relationships.

The community may also include some members who have not developed a capacity for intimacy. Such people have an unclear sense of identity that does not make mutuality possible. Given this range of needs and expectations, some general discussion of expectations of community interactions and relationships is helpful. As time passes and relationships shift, there may be need for further discussion and clarification.

## Spectrum of Relationships

The scope and range of intimate relationships is wide and depends on the trust level, knowledge of the other, and the choice of closeness desired. Relationships are by their very nature mutual, so the level of intimacy is of utmost importance. Forced intimacy invades privacy, contradicts personal freedom, and leads to a draining and unproductive relationship. Mutuality and reciprocity are key elements in relationships.

In every life there are myriad relationships. These relationships are not identical in importance, duration, consistency, quality, depth, affection, or intensity. The levels of intimacy in this spectrum are not equal, nor should there be a desire to have the same level of intimacy for every relationship. The terms used to describe a relationship frequently denote it's level, ranging from acquaintance to one's closest confidant. For example, one can have: a passing acquaintance with the daily postal carrier, a professional relationship with the medical doctor, a business relationship with a work colleague, a close relationship with a friend, a limited friendship with a community member, a loving relationship with a spouse.

A healthy individual has many people from whom to draw. These people form a person's support network and are available to support the different aspects of one's life. They provide positive resources in times of crisis as well as a necessary context to maintain a healthy way of life.

### Table 12.1
# Relationship Circles

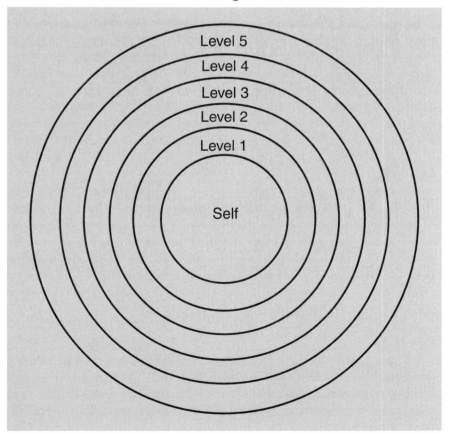

The concentric circles in Table 12.1 represent the different levels of intimacy. The center circle symbolizes the self. The outside circles show the degree of relationship by their proximity to the center. Each person has to choose where they would place the individual members of their community, as well as the community as a whole.

## Level 5

This is the level furthest away from the self. People in this category know the basic data: name, occupation, history, background. This group has only surface knowledge of you. An acquaintance relationship may develop from some common association. This group usually contains the largest number of people.

## Level 4

People in this category share some common bond. In addition to knowing some of the basic facts about you, the individuals in this level know some of your opinions and ideas. There is sharing at this level, but it is usually related to the common bond, such as among professional or work colleagues, AA members, parish coworkers, neighbors, social contacts. This group contains fewer people than Level 5.

## Level 3

The number of people in this circle is becoming fewer. Though they may have the same common bond as some in Level 4, you have chosen to share more of self with these people. Of course, they have the same knowledge as the individuals in the previous two levels, but in somewhat more depth. Mutual sharing of beliefs, attitudes, values, and a spiritual dimension has begun to occur. This group may be comprised of colleagues, family members, associates from civic, religious, or parent organizations, neighbors, social contacts. These people could be considered distant friends.

## Level 2

Besides the quality sharing of values, attitudes, and beliefs, there is also a selective sharing of feelings and emotions at this level, a trust and comfort level that permits the revealing of the faith dimension to an even greater depth. There is an obviously smaller number of individuals that will be allowed into this circle. These people are considered close friends. At this level there is increased vulnerability. The material about oneself that is shared conveys a sense of trust in the other.

## Level 1

Though the deepest and richest level of relationship, Level 1 contains the smallest number of individuals. At this circle a high level of trust exists, and there is a willingness to share the deepest part, almost everything, about oneself. This degree of vulnerability is risked because of the strong belief in the other person. This level of intimacy is special and reserved for very close friends. It may include one or two friends in a lifetime who are in this circle.

## Fears of Intimacy

While the human need for intimacy is universally present, there is also the risk of vulnerability that can pose a threat and can stimulate fear. Fears of intimacy can take different forms, as Table 12.2 illustrates.

### Table 12.2
### Fears of Intimacy

1. Fear of rejection and ridicule
2. Misuse of power
3. Lack of mutuality
4. Fear of termination

Two of the more common fears are those of rejection and ridicule. Every person has a basic desire to be loved and accepted. The attempt to relate to another can be accompanied with the unspoken question as to whether this action will be accepted or will be met with rejection or ridicule. This fear can be particularly strong for individuals whose self-esteem is low and who may have difficulty in seeing themselves as acceptable and lovable.

Once the risk to share something of oneself with another is taken, this knowledge places that person in a position of power. If there is some disruption or misunderstanding in the relationship, there can be a fear that the information will be used maliciously.

Another fear stems from the mutuality that is the expectation in any relationship. The question that self-disclosure may not be reciprocated or that one is being used solely to fill another person's need can be a cause of fear.

Last, the reality of termination which is a constant in a community can make it difficult for individuals to build relationships. This fear points to the importance of a community addressing the departure of members from the community as discussed in chapter 1 and in chapter 13. When members can process their feelings of loss and separation, they can overcome more easily their fear of loss and can be free to form new relationships.

The fears of intimacy are numerous and individual. They may change according to the circumstances, and one can experience different fears with different persons. A key factor in establishing relationships is knowledge of one's personal fears that may hinder developing intimacy.

## Defenses Against Intimacy

There are times and circumstances when fears of intimacy can become too great, and the need to protect oneself from a perceived threat prevails. A person then engages in behaviors called "defenses" that serve to protect and defend the self.

Among the more commonly-known defenses are workaholism and intellectualization. For example, some people can become so totally consumed in their work that they have no time or interest in any other aspect of life. By complete absorption in work they can avoid interacting on a personal basis. In a similar vein, focusing on facts, data, and information may be a screen to hide one's real self from others. This defense of intellectualization is recognized when the only possible conversations with some people are about sports, events, news, and other impersonal facts.

Among the other defenses are: pseudo-asceticism, where God and "holy talk" become an escape; pseudo-professionalism, which hides behind a role; or various types of obsession such as with pets and humor.

Most people utilize defenses periodically or situationally, and it is not problematic. However, whenever defenses become the norm for interacting, they impede individual growth and inhibit building community.

## Summary

Within every human person there is a hunger for intimacy and a need to be connected in some way with others. Growth as human persons is through relationship with others. Created as social beings, there is a need to interact with others. Through interactions and relationships individuals grow more fully into the person God calls them to become.

Intimacy is the capacity to allow oneself to be known by others and to know others in return. While the desire for intimacy exists, there is also an accompanying reluctance. When the threat to one's vulnerability is too great, a person employs defenses which establish behaviors that prevent developing relationships, whether in family, community, work, or social settings.

In every life there is a variety of types of relationships. The degree of intimacy varies according to the type of relationship and the mutual choice of both parties. Within community there will also be a range of relationship levels.

Members of a community bring with them varying needs and expectations of intimacy. Finding a level of intimacy that is acceptable and comfortable for all has to be negotiated if the group is to form community. The challenge is a difficult but necessary one if the community is to move toward its purpose and mission.

## Suggested Readings

Juliano, Carroll and Loughlan Sofield, "Ministry Demands Intimacy," *Human Development*, Vol. 9 #1, Spring 1988, pp. 31-34.

Livingston, Patricia. *Lessons of the Heart*. Notre Dame, IN: Ave Maria Press, 1992.

## Reflection Questions

1. What is the place of intimacy in my life?
2. Which are my most common fears of intimacy? Are these fears different with different individuals?
3. When I experience a need to protect myself, which defenses do I employ?
4. What are my expectations for intimacy in our community?

## Process for Group Sharing

1. Review the levels of relationships in Table 12.1. Using the sections on Worksheet 12.A, identify individuals you would place at each level.
2. Reflect on the following questions:

   Where did you place the members in your community?

   Is it different from where you would prefer to place them?

   Is there anyone who seems to desire a closer relationship to you than you choose to have?

   Is there anyone in your life now that you would place in Level 1?

   What are the expectations of intimacy that I hold for this community?
3. As a community, discuss your response to the final question.

# Relationship Circles

Refer to Table 12.1 and the description of the relationships on each level. Then place the names of individuals at each level.

Level 5

Level 4

Level 3

Level 2

Level 1

# 13

# Termination and Loss: A Cause of Anxiety in Community

*Then all the disciples deserted him and ran away.*

*—Matthew 26:56*

Both Matthew and Mark relate the disciples' retreat quoted above. This straightforward declaration stands starkly as an isolated fact, almost interrupting the natural flow of the passion narrative. The disciples' behavior occurs immediately after Jesus is arrested. The response of the disciples is the communal reaction of an anxious group who anticipate the loss of their revered leader. Woven through the narrative of the arrest of Jesus is the description of some bizarre behavior on the part of these disciples. There is the almost amusing description of the young man shedding his garment and running away naked. At a time when it would seem the disciples would be more concerned about relevant and pressing issues, the reader finds the disciples discussing who is the greatest among them. Peter, as the new designated leader, seems to epitomize this strange behavior. He engages in rash, violent behavior by cutting off a man's ear! Peter is also observed sitting by a fire, not only denying Jesus but also becoming extremely hostile in the process. He seems to be experiencing wild mood swings. At one moment Peter is assertive and aggressive. In the next moment he is a weepy, guilt-ridden follower of Jesus. Describing the behavior of these committed disciples as bizarre is indeed an understatement.

The behavior manifested by the disciples is a fairly predictable dynamic that occurs in most groups and communities. When an ending, a transition, or a termination is approaching, a community that has been functioning productively and maturely often displays seemingly bizarre and immature behavior. Group members find themselves surprised, confused, embarrassed, and bewildered by their erratic behavior but feel incapable of changing it. The question that arises for both participants and observers is, "How can adults who function at a mature level suddenly become adolescent and even childish in their behavior?" This behavioral change is a normal dynamic that is evident in most groups when there is transition and/or termination. At times of separation, termination, and loss, each community member and the community as a whole experience anxiety. Anxiety triggers bizarre and regressive behavior. This behavior serves as a defense against confronting the difficult and often painful emotional reactions to loss.

The catalysts that produce these reactions can be multiple. One possibility occurs when the community, as it presently exists, is coming to an end at the actual termination of the entire group. Another possibility can happen when the community changes composition. Perhaps a new member is added to the group, or a member departs. Whenever any change of membership occurs, the group becomes a new entity, a new community, and the shift in composition triggers the dynamic of loss. Regardless of the cause of change, the group can anticipate anxiety and may encounter bizarre behavior.

There is pain present in any loss, even losses that seem relatively inconsequential. The pain exists because the human psyche never completely finishes grieving over previous significant losses. These significant losses can be varied: the death of a loved one; alienation from a significant person; or the losses experienced in the ordinary transitions of life, such as graduation, relocation, or retirement. Whenever loss is experienced, the process of grieving commences. However, grieving is so painful that the normal, self-protecting reaction is to curtail the process. The result is "unfinished business." The incomplete grieving is stored within the recesses of an individual's psyche. Therefore, any subsequent losses, terminations, or separations resurrect the unfinished business. Each new loss is experienced both as a painful feeling of loss in the present and a reworking of the stored pain of the past. It is not surprising that communities expend much energy avoiding the process and dynamics of loss. The avoidance is usually more unconscious than conscious.

The normal reaction to loss is denial. Denial is employed as a defense because the community wants to avoid the painful memories associated with previous significant losses. Often there is an unconscious collusion among members to avoid facing the reality of loss. In fact, any member who challenges the group to address the reality of loss will frequently become scapegoated by the community. Scapegoating is a normal group defense to avoid anxiety-producing issues. It is a process in which the group denies its own limitations and projects blame for anything negative onto a single member of the group. The members then attempt to drive that member from the group. Unconsciously, there is hope of dispelling the "evil" within the group. Therefore, the responsible member who calls the community to look at the "evil" of its pain is targeted as scapegoat.

Defenses, such as scapegoating, are destructive to the community and often are debilitating for the individuals who consume much psychic energy in the process. Defenses often retard the emotional growth of the members and the community.

Terminations of any nature are especially significant for women. Maggie Scarff, in *Unfinished Business: Pressure Points in the Lives of Women*, suggests that when women enter into relationships, they often allow others to become so much a part of them that egos overlap and merge. As a result, when women undergo loss, separation, or termination they experience not only a loss of the other, but also a part of themselves, their ego, dies in the process. Thus termination is generally more profound for women than for men.

Very sensitive men may experience a similar but less intense reaction than women. A twenty-year study of those who have taken the 16 PF, a personality profile, discovered that priests differed from other men in that they were more "tender-minded." Tender-minded means that they are more gentle, caring, and emotionally sensitive. In addition, there is a greater need to be appreciated, valued, and needed. Consequently, we believe that any tender-minded male may experience termination as women do.

## Six Steps for Managing Loss

Dealing with termination is a difficult process. Ignoring termination often retards the individual's capacity to invest in new relationships and new communities. In your present community, how do you handle the saying of good-byes? We suggest six steps as necessary for any community to manage losses and endings more effectively.

### Table 13.1
## Six Steps in Dealing With Loss/Termination

1. Get in touch with all the emotions you are experiencing.
2. Accept the feelings.
3. Talk about the feeling.
4. Allow sufficient time to grieve.
5. Ritualize the loss.
6. Allow new people to enter your life.

### Step 1: Acknowledge all the emotions you are experiencing.

This is often more difficult than it might appear. For many persons, identifying their feelings is a difficult task. At times of loss a wide spectrum of feelings and emotions from extreme sadness to utter relief emerges. But one emotion inevitably surfaces at this time, and it is anger. Emotions that are considered "taboo," inappropriate, or unchristian are generally suppressed or repressed. Is it acceptable for you to feel a wide range of emotions? Are there some emotions that are taboo? Are you comfortable feeling anger at times of loss? The range of emotions experienced at times of loss are like layers of an onion. As each layer is peeled away another appears. The same is true for the strata of emotions. Some emotions are very apparent, easily recognized, and readily acknowledged, but the emotions that are perceived as negative or painful are the most difficult to identify and embrace.

### Step 2: Accept the feelings.

Identifying feelings is only a first step. The next and more difficult task is to accept and embrace these feelings. In particular, those emotions that are considered taboo produce anxiety when one tries to confront them. Anxiety, in turn, agitates a person's defenses, impeding growth in self-knowledge and self-acceptance. Can you acknowledge, accept, and even embrace the emotions you have labeled as "negative"? Can you give yourself permission to feel angry, sad, depressed, jealous, relieved, etc.?

### Step 3: Talk about the feeling.

Talking about feelings is not an easy task for communities. The verbal acknowledgment of the present loss serves as a catalyst in unearthing the painful unfinished grieving that had been stored in the individual's psyche. Talking about one's feelings raises stored grieving to consciousness. A person, then, will expend great energy to prevent its emergence. An unconscious conspiracy to avoid discussing an issue that could give rise to the suppressed pain can exist in communities. The very act of listening to another talk of the pain of loss can give rise to the hearer's suppressed grieving. Once the resistance is overcome, then the community can move beyond merely listening to validating the feelings that have been expressed. The validation of feelings serves as a catharsis and creates the climate and conditions to engage in further dialogue.

### Step 4: Allow sufficient time to grieve.

Grieving is a critical step in the process of loss. No two people have identical, incomplete grieving issues, and no two people will require the same amount of time to grieve. There is no universal method for grieving. Each person's method will be unique to her or him. The amount of grieving an individual must do depends on a number of factors. How much stored grieving is accumulated? How is self-esteem affected by this loss? How many losses are experienced in a relatively short time? Research indicates that one of the greatest causes of stress in life is the experience of separation, termination, or loss. Multiple losses can have not only psychological repercussions, but physiological ones. Failure to grieve adequately will cause both emotional and bodily harm.

## Step 5: Ritualize the loss.

Besides speaking of loss, it is important to find significant ways to ritualize it. Ritual provides another vehicle for "speaking" the reality of loss. The rituals used must give voice to the members of the community in a profound way. Ritualizing, like grieving, cannot be artificial. The methods for ritualizing must be appropriate and significant for the group members. In our experience, the ability to develop appropriate rituals is a rare gift not possessed by all. We suggest that a community discerns who has that gift and delegates that person to develop appropriate and meaningful rituals for the community. Failure to engage in adequate grieving and ritualization significantly curtails the process of dealing effectively with termination.

## Step 6: Allow new people to enter your life.

Christians are death/resurrection people. Only when we enter into our death experiences, our losses, do we free ourselves to experience the joy of resurrection. A community that refrains from entering into the process of dying and grieving is incapable of experiencing the resurrection, the new, divine life.

Adhering to these six steps will not make termination and grieving easy. Termination is a very difficult and often painful process. Omitting the process of termination will have severe negative repercussions not only on the continued growth of the current members but also on future members. The dynamic of termination and loss is a reality for all communities. In working with communities we have discovered that this dynamic is rarely addressed in a way which is life-giving for the community.

## Summary

The experience of termination, separation, or loss is a normal stage in the life of every community. Many communities fail to be life-giving for their members because they find the process of grieving and managing loss too painful. Only those communities that are mature enough to enter into the process of dying will provide the necessary regeneration in the lives of their members. A community can take positive steps that will lead to a successful resolution of this stage.

## Suggested Readings

Myers, Isabel Briggs. *Introduction to Type*. Consulting Psychologists Press, Inc., 1980.

Rupp, Joyce. *Praying Our Goodbyes*. Notre Dame, IN: Ave Maria Press, 1988.

Scarff, Maggie. *Unfinished Business: Pressure Points in the Lives of Women*. Garden City, NY: Doubleday, 1980.

Sofield, Loughlan and Rosine Hammett, "Experiencing Termination in Community," *Human Development*, Vol. 2, No. 2, Summer 1981, pp. 24-31.

Viorst, Judith. *Necessary Losses*. New York: Simon and Schuster, 1986.

## Reflection Questions

1. What terminations, separations, and losses have we experienced in our community?
2. How have we dealt with these issues?
3. What "unfinished business" continues to influence or dominate our communal life today, and what can we do to rectify this?

## Process for Group Sharing

### Process #1

1. Reflect on the major losses you have experienced in life. Using the six steps suggested above, determine how you have managed your losses.
2. As a community, focus on the community losses you have experienced. Discuss the positive and negative ways in which the losses were managed. Determine if the "unfinished business" is interfering with the growth and development of the community. If so, determine what steps you will take to remedy this.
3. Sometimes, when people end their membership in community, they give a reason that sounds very appropriate and "nice." We encourage communities to conduct a form of "exit interview." This provides the community with a forum for feedback on why they may not be attracting or retaining members. Most groups are reluctant to receive this type of feedback, but ultimately it can provide valuable data for the community to make necessary adjustments.

## Process #2

1. Use Worksheet 13.A for reflection and as an exercise.
2. Identify major experiences of loss, transition, and termination that you have had personally in life.
3. Identify major experiences of loss, transition, and termination that have been experienced by the community.
4. Reflect on each of these situations:
   a) Use the six steps recommended for dealing with termination.
   b) Identify where that has been unfinished business for you and/or the community.
   c) Focus on the possible effects and impact this loss has on you and the community.

# Worksheet 13.A

1. Community losses

2. Positive ways these were managed

3. Negative ways these were managed

4. What has not been dealt with?

5. How will we do this?

# Reflections on Experiences of Transition, Loss, and Termination

| Experiences of loss, transition, and termination | Unfinished business | Possible impact on me personally | Possible impact on our communal life, dynamics, and relationships |
|---|---|---|---|
| **Personal** | | | |
| 1. | | | |
| 2. | | | |
| 3. | | | |
| **Communal** | | | |
| 1. | | | |
| 2. | | | |
| 3. | | | |

# 14
## Listening

*Speak, Yahweh; for your servant is listening.*
*—1 Samuel 3:10*

An article in a psychiatric journal reported the story of a man whose wife was hospitalized for depression. She was Asian and not fluent in English. The psychiatrist assigned as her therapist saw her for an hour session, three times a week for six weeks. The woman and the psychiatrist did not speak the same language. Given the circumstances, the therapy seemed doomed to failure.

However, at the end of six weeks the husband appeared in the doctor's office and declared that his wife was no longer depressed. The husband asked what approach the psychiatrist used to achieve this almost miraculous effect. The psychiatrist replied that he had simply listened to the woman and attempted to understand what it must be like to be in her situation. Although he could not understand her words, he could hear the pain, the confusion, the depression, and the hopelessness she was conveying with her whole being. He was successful because he listened to more than just words, and he conveyed to her his understanding of her pain and his concern for her.

## Listening as a Therapeutic and Healing Process

Listening to members of community in the same way the psychiatrist listened to the depressed woman creates a climate that is healing and therapeutic. Every person longs to be heard, to be understood, to be accepted, and to be loved. The process of listening creates the conditions and the climate where these longings and needs are satisfied. The act of listening with an attempt to understand another creates not only a healthy climate but also a holy space. In order to achieve this, the listener must attend to the other with an open heart, desirous of encountering the other in a new way. This is not an easy task since most people listen out of their own predetermined images formed from previous experiences with other persons.

## Listening as a Skill

Listening is a skill. As with most skills, it may not come easily or naturally, but it can be learned. First of all, it is a matter of paying attention, of disciplining ourselves to stay focused on the other who is speaking. It is so easy to get distracted, to begin to fashion a response in one's own mind, or to assume that we know everything the person is going to say from the little we have heard. A good listener not only has the patience to stay with the speaker as he or she communicates what is to be said, but also has an interest in the other, a desire to know and understand what is being said.

The skill of listening calls for receiving the message being communicated, but it also involves letting the speaker know that we are receiving the message. We let the other know that we are listening by making eye contact, by taking an open and receptive posture, and when appropriate, by offering simple verbal affirmations such as "uh-huh" or "ahh."

Listening requires an effort born of interest, concern, and love. It goes beyond merely receiving words from another. The psychiatrist described above had the capacity to listen in a way that communicated how much he cared. He heard more than just words that were, in themselves, unintelligible to him. True listening transcends words to arrive at the unspoken heart and mind of the other.

Reflective listening is an approach pioneered by the psychiatrist Carl Rogers. Like the psychiatrist in the story above, Rogers believed in the healing power of listening. His aim as a listener was to reflect back to the speaker what was being said. In response to a statement like, "I was very hurt when the group forgot the anniversary of my wife's death," a reflective listener might say, "That really must have been painful for you." Reflective listening lets the speaker know that you have heard what is being said and offers the opportunity and encouragement to say still more.

A possible pitfall in reflective listening is that it can sometimes sound artificial. The simple repetition of the speaker's words can come across in a negative way unless the listener conveys that more than the words are being heard. A good listener will indicate to the speaker not only a comprehension of words, but also the comprehension of the profound communication expressed in those words. Active listening is a wonderful skill, but only when the listener comprehends the latent content, i.e., the emotions and passion that exist beyond the words.

## Listening as an Attitude

Acquiring the tools and skills for listening is important. Of even greater significance is developing an attitude of listening. Communication meets with success only when an attitude of concern and interest in the other is conveyed. Thus, forming an attitude of listening is of greater consequence than just the possession of communication tools and skills. A person who is an effective listener is able to "touch" another by understanding what the other is trying to communicate even when the speaker may not be fully aware of his or her own message. This profound listening is transmitted often by a "listening presence" that frees the other to risk sharing ideas, thoughts, and feelings which might be threatening and scary. An attitude of a "listening presence" can be nurtured and perfected. This attitude is exemplified in a man whose acquaintances describe an encounter with him as a "sacramental moment." In speaking with him, people not only feel heard, listened to, and understood, but also find their self-esteem enhanced. Something in his listening presence leaves the other experiencing a sense of personal value. He listens and hears people at many different levels, even levels they are unaware of.

## Learning to Listen on Many Levels

Communication transpires on many levels, and not all communication is direct. Direct communication of words conveys one message, but indirect communication of meaning often conveys a deeper message. Those who listen too literally to the words may miss the message. Truly effective listeners hear not only the manifest content or the actual words but also the latent content or the layers of indirect communication. They can grasp the symbolism used to convey intense, powerful, and, at times, fear-filled messages.

During a workshop on transition, termination, and loss, a recent immigrant from Ireland asked the assembled group if they knew what he missed most about his homeland. Not waiting for a response, he stated with tears in his eyes, "A good potato!" On the surface his comment sounded humorous, but he was actually communicating an intense, underlying feeling. What he was trying to convey was very meaningful for him. For a person of Irish heritage, the potato represents and symbolizes a period in Irish history when whole families died as a result of the potato famine. Relatives emigrated from a country that could no longer produce their primary food staple. Families were separated, and some of those families never reunited. To be an effective listener, one must learn to listen with the heart and identify the symbols below the surface of the words.

In addition, sometimes effective listening employs "the gut." At times a speaker may be unaware that he or she is conveying a message in such a way that the listener can "feel" it, even before the words are articulated. Part of the skill of listening is knowing those situations and times when it becomes necessary to disengage from the manifest content and pay close attention to the emotional response. At these times the skilled listener disconnects from attending to the spoken words and asks, "What am I feeling and why am I feeling this? Is this feeling part of my own reaction, or am I sensing an emotional, nonverbal signal from the other?" In these cases, focusing on the words becomes a major obstacle to authentic listening. Those who listen too literally often miss the powerful messages being communicated and conveyed through symbol and silence.

Listening to silence is a valuable skill that facilitates communication in community. However, silence can be interpreted prematurely or inaccurately. All behavior is multi-causal. Silence can have many different meanings. A moment of silence in a community can communicate fear, profound reflection, agreement, or disagreement. No assumptions should be made as to the meaning of silence or whether silence means the same thing to each person. The skillful listener asks questions for clarification and makes no assumptions.

## Table 14.1
## Levels of Listening

Listening to words for content and meaning
Identifying the symbols within the words
Noticing your own emotional response
Interpreting silence

## Obstacles to Listening

There is no perfect listener. Even when the desire to be a good listener is present, there can be personal obstacles that interfere. These obstacles are multifaceted and include past histories, needs, fears, and too-literal listening as described earlier.

At times the inability to listen in the present is related to the past. Past events and encounters can invade the present and distract from the present moment. "Elephant memories," recollections of past encounters, can prevent a person from listening anew. Every person can identify times of "shutting down" when someone is talking. Based on previous experiences with the speaker we presume to know what the person is going to say, so we do not listen to what is being conveyed in the present, but play our own tapes from the past. Once stereotyping occurs it becomes difficult to see people as they are. Stereotyping denies that people can change, even though each new experience creates a new person with different ideas, ideals, and values. The wisdom of the other is denied you because you have made yourself incapable of hearing anything other than what was expected to be heard. As a result, you live with the members of the community of the past: you deny yourself the joy of encountering the new people constantly unfolding and being revealed in your midst.

You may also have been on the receiving end of this stereotyping and "elephant memories," experiencing utter frustration because of the inability of the others to hear what you are saying because they are judging you on what you have previously said. They hear the present communication only through the prism of their past experiences with you.

Whom do you find it difficult to listen to in your community? Who have you so stereotyped so that you no longer can listen or hear them? Can you change the filters through which you screen the words and messages of your community members? At the next communal gathering will you evaluate your openness and ability to listen to each person, especially those you find most difficult?

Another obstacle to listening is one's own personal needs. Since most behavior is need-driven, the answer to understanding one's behavior lies in recognizing the need that produces that behavior. This is especially true when the message being sent would threaten a fragile self-esteem.

A third obstacle to communication and listening is the listener's fear. There are many fears that may be operative. There may be fear of the pain of the challenge to change that might result if what is being said is really heard. The fear may also be a fear of hearing things that are unpleasant or the fear that better communication will lead to conflict.

Each person in the community is challenged to identify his or her own personal blocks to listening. Individual self-awareness is the first step in the overcoming of personal obstacles to listening. When people are able to overcome these emotionally paralyzing blocks, they are freed to listen and love in a new way.

Thomas Morgan writes:

> Karl Menninger believed that the experience of not being listened to made people unwell, and the experience of being listened to made them well again. The experience of being loved through listening made them whole again . . . Listening is the heart of ministry.[1]

When we listen, we affirm and empower the other. Our listening is a gift to the other. When we don't listen, we fail to hear the Spirit being revealed through others, and we impede the development of life in the members and in the community.

Douglas Steere states: "To 'listen' another's soul into a condition of disclosure and discovery may be almost the greatest service that any human being ever performs for another."

## Summary

Listening creates a climate in communities where people feel understood, accepted, and loved. Listening is a skill that challenges us to focus on hearing the other at different levels. Ears are only one organ for listening and hearing. We must listen with our hearts and with our "gut." Those who wish to develop greater skill in listening need to identify the obstacles within themselves that interfere with their ability to listen to others in the community.

## Suggested Readings

Juliano, Carroll and Loughlan Sofield, "A Model for Evaluating Communication," *Review for Religious*, Vol. 44, #5, Sept./Oct. 1985, pp. 694-703.

McNerney, Eileen, "Deciding Community Life's Future," *Human Development*, Vol. 14 #3, Fall 1993, pp. 10-14.

Sofield, Loughlan, Carroll Juliano, and Rosine Hammett. *Design for Wholeness: Dealing with Anger, Learning to Forgive and Building Self Esteem.* Notre Dame, IN: Ave Maria Press, 1990, pp. 111-143.

Tennebaum, Deborah. *You Just Don't Understand Me.* New York: Ballantine, 1990.

Walchars, John. *Resurrection of Values.* New York: Crossroad, 1986, chapter 10.

## Reflection Questions

1. When was a time when I truly felt listened to? Recall the incident and identify what helped create the listening climate. What does this experience say to me about developing my own skills and attitudes of listening?
2. What is my major obstacle to really listening to the people in my community?
3. What are the times or circumstances when listening to community members is a real challenge?

## Process for Group Sharing

1. One member prepares a prayer service to help create a climate to facilitate listening.
2. Each person chooses one of the selected readings and reflects on the above questions.
3. Each member shares his or her reaction to this chapter and the readings.
4. The session concludes with prayer.

# 15
# *Emotions:*
# *Avenues to Growth*

*And he began to feel terror and anguish.*
*—Mark 14:34*

Love, happiness, joy, peacefulness, fear, anxiety, hate, envy, jealousy, sadness, anger, rage. . . . These emotions are common to everyone. Each of the words may evoke a different reaction, extending from mild to strong, from positive to negative. Emotions in themselves, however, are neutral, neither negative nor positive. The negative or positive value of an emotion is added by each person based on personal beliefs and experiences. Emotions serve as triggers; they stimulate a reaction within a person. For example, a positive connotation might be attached to *love* based on one's experience of that emotion in the past. However, if one's desire for love has been constantly frustrated or rejected, or there has not been an experience of love, then *love* might have a negative connotation. Reading *jealousy* could trigger a negative feeling because of a belief that jealousy has no place in the life of a good person. On the other hand, if being jealous of someone's gift spurred a person to develop a particular gift in himself or herself, then *jealousy* might not be viewed in a totally negative light.

## The Effect of Emotions on Community

Emotions have an vital and pivotal role to play in the life of every person and every community. Beyond the natural psychological realm, emotions are God-given vehicles to facilitate growth in the Christian life. Emotions also play a central role in the life and growth of community. To the degree that members feel comfortable with the variety and multiplicity of their emotions and those of other members, emotions will contribute to the growth of community. The following example highlights this.

The staff of a parish that was organized around a model of small Christian communities was meeting with the leaders of the

155

communities to monitor their development. One of the leaders reported on a unique experience that had occurred in their community.

The group had been characterized by a paralyzing fear. One of the members of the group was prone to extreme mood swings. At times he would completely dominate the meetings. At other times he would be irrational and belligerent.

Some of the members became annoyed, not only with him, but with themselves for allowing this erratic behavior to control them. They talked privately about their fear and decided to openly discuss their reactions and emotions at the next meeting. The offending person immediately expressed his relief at discussing his behavior in the community. He mentioned that he had been under the care of a psychiatrist and was taking medication that played havoc with his emotions. He often felt emotionally out of control and thanked the community for their concern and care.

Initially, the community allowed itself to be paralyzed by the emotion of fear. Once they confronted the emotion and decided to deal with it in an honest and mature way, it had beneficial results for the individual concerned and the entire community.

The way in which members accept, process, and express emotions has a profound impact on community. The normal dynamics occurring within community stimulate various emotions. When members fear the presence of any emotion, the focus of the group can shift to that emotion, thus diverting the group. For example, a member who shows anger may become the center of attention, and the group unconsciously works toward keeping the member happy. The community's energy, whether spent in denial or avoidance, is drained away from the work. Decisions made at this time can be swayed by the emotional tenor of the group rather than based on objective data. Inadvertently, a community can move away from its purpose and goals and allow itself to be led by the uncontrolled emotional responses of its members.

## Beliefs About Emotions

Table 15.1 offers readers the opportunity to reflect on their beliefs about emotions.

### Table 15.1
### Beliefs About Emotions

1. Emotions provide powerful clues to what is transpiring in both the human and communal system.
2. Emotions have a strong effect on behavior.
3. Emotions are produced by beliefs and images.
4. Emotions are neither positive nor negative.
5. Emotions are either pleasant or painful.
6. Emotions are not sinful.
7. Emotions do not dictate or control behavior.
8. Certain emotions are more fear-producing, especially for some people.

Emotions provide clear, intense, and often insightful clues to what is transpiring in one's inner and outer worlds. Emotions are a potential source for developing self-knowledge. They also frequently furnish the energy to move one to action. Emotions might move one into relationships. They may warn one about a threat to one's person, security, or safety. They can provide the stimulus to overcome unjust situations. Emotions are gifts from God providing opportunities for growth.

However, their intensity and the moral evaluation one places on them can have the opposite effect. In such cases, emotions might produce fear, inertia, retreat, or paralysis. For example, if you entered the vermin-infected home of someone living in squalor, you would probably experience a host of emotions, including revulsion, fear, anger, and empathy. The combination of these emotions can lead to a variety of behaviors. On the one hand, you might find yourself escaping to a place that provides more comfort and ease. Or, your emotions could influence your behavior in an entirely different way, giving you the energy to take positive steps to change the inhuman situation.

We recently encountered two people who visited a hospice ministering to people with AIDS. Both individuals experienced almost identical emotions, similar to the mixture of emotions felt by the person in the example above. The first person, who took time to process her emotions, made a choice to become directly involved in working with people with AIDS and began to discern ways to educate and involve others. The second person became a victim of those emotions. She experienced an overwhelming sense of powerlessness and made an almost unconscious decision to never return to the hospice again. She failed to enter into the emotion and, as a result, it had a negative effect on her.

## Value of Emotions

Emotions are signs of life. They provide clues as to what is happening in one's internal and external life. Emotions help in reading and interpreting the experiences of daily life. Emotions are pointers that help a person to make sense out of what is happening in his or her inner life. Emotions can help to understand the world around us. There are myriad encounters and events that occur in the daily circumstances of life. Tapping into emotions can aid in processing the external world and its impact on a person. Thus emotions help us to understand ourselves and others and can assist in building more effective and life-giving communities.

**Table 15.2**
# Value of Emotions

1. Embracing each individual emotion frees you to experience a wider range of emotions.
2. Identifying and acknowledging your own emotions sensitizes you and makes you more empathetic to others.
3. Reflecting on emotions provides an assortment of responses other than merely reacting.
4. Accepting emotions strengthens your resolve and will.
5. Admitting your own emotions frees you from being overly-influenced by the emotions of others.
6. Being in touch with emotions provides additional opportunities to experience love, joy, excitement, passion, zeal, etc.
7. Understanding one's emotions enhances the possibility for improving relationships.

## Capacity to Process Emotions

In the course of each day we are bombarded with myriad experiences that stimulate our emotions. When we are in touch with these emotions, we are better able to understand our connectedness to the world; there is an opportunity to look at the experience and learn from it. This gives us greater sense of control of who we are and keeps us from being controlled by circumstances or others. When we are comfortable experiencing emotions, we have a greater sense of security. The fear of being controlled by our emotions is absent, as is the fear that others or others' reactions will exert control.

Unfortunately, not every person accepts the wide range of emotions that are part of the human condition. Thus not everyone is capable of using these triggers for growth. For some, the world of feelings and emotions seems out of reach, while others are overpowered and paralyzed by them. Still others find feelings and emotions are very present, but they choose to deny them. Emotions can only be channels of growth and agents of change when a person has the ability first to experience an emotion, then internalize it, and finally, learn from it.

The capacity to process emotions is learned and conditioned by family, society, and culture. Coming from one's learned history, emotions can be viewed as a gift from God to help us grow in personhood, or as an evil temptation that, when experienced, detract and denigrate one's self.

## Decisions Regarding Emotions

Ultimately, only the person experiencing the emotion has the power to determine how it will be expressed. He or she also has control, to a great extent, over what emotions will perdure. Emotions are feelings. Feelings that continue for extended periods produce moods. Emotions arise as spontaneous internal reactions to an internal (beliefs, perceptions, or images) or external stimulus. While we have little control over when and how our emotions begin, most people have control over whether an emotion will persist as a mood. The person experiencing the emotion, especially one arising from an internal stimulus, can choose which pictures (beliefs, perceptions, or images) to run in the cinema of the mind. You are your own projectionist. The pictures you choose to run in your own mind determine the emotions and moods you will experience. Someone, for instance, who has had a violent argument with a friend or spouse has choices. What do you choose to focus on: the present painful experience or the years of beautiful friendship?

There are at least two major choices available to you, if you wish to change your emotions:

Change the situation. Sometimes that means removing yourself from the circumstances which produce the emotion. This is appropriate when the situation is one that you are unable to change and produces an inordinate and unhealthy amount of frustration and anger.

Or you can change your beliefs, perceptions, or images. Chapter 3 described the relationships between beliefs and emotions. What you feel is determined by how you perceive or what you believe about a person or situation. Realize that you, as the projectionist of your own perceptions, choose which images you wish to project on your own mind and heart.

## The Role of Emotions in Community

Any community is a compilation of individuals with differing backgrounds, personal histories, personality traits, and characteristics. Here are a number of ways in which emotions influence the life and development of community, either positively or negatively.

### Table 15.3
## Role of Emotion in a Community

1. Emotions that are unacknowledged usually come out in indirect and destructive ways.
2. Communal behavior or decisions that are determined solely on the basis of emotions will usually be inappropriate and/or ineffective decisions.
3. Communities that acknowledge and allow the appropriate expressions of emotions have the potential to become vital and energizing communities.
4. Communities that encourage the expression of emotions will create a climate where people can feel loved, accepted, and challenged.

## Summary

Emotions have a vital and pivotal role to play in the life of every person and community. The way members accept, process, and express emotions has a profound effect on community. Emotions provide important clues to what is occurring in the internal and external lives of both individual members and the community as a whole.

## Suggested Reading

Padovani, Martin H. *Healing Wounded Emotions*. Mystic, CT: Twenty-Third Publications, 1990.

## Reflection Questions

1. What are some of the strongest feelings I have encountered in community during the last few days? What do these feelings say to me about what is happening within me and in my relationships?
2. Do I accept or deny my emotions? Which emotions do I value? Which ones do I shun? Am I happy with the way I express them, or would I prefer to develop different responses?

## Process for Group Sharing

Worksheet 15.A contains a list of the more common emotions. Read each emotion and indicate how you value this emotion in your life. Is it a "positive" emotion that you will allow yourself to experience? Is it a negative or unacceptable emotion for you? Is it an emotion that you will not allow yourself to experience and therefore deny its existence? What is your reaction when others express this emotion?

# Worksheet 15.A

| Emotion | Immediate Reaction | Strength of Reaction | Personal Implications | Implications for Communal Life |
| --- | --- | --- | --- | --- |
| Love | | | | |
| Happiness | | | | |
| Joy | | | | |
| Peacefulness | | | | |
| Fear | | | | |
| Anxiety | | | | |
| Hate | | | | |
| Envy | | | | |
| Jealousy | | | | |
| Sadness | | | | |
| Anger | | | | |
| Rage | | | | |

# 16
## Confrontation: Difficult but Essential

*If your brother does something wrong, go
and have it out with him alone, between
your two selves.*
                    *—Matthew 18:15*

One of the most difficult tasks in community is confrontation. And for most community members, it is an underdeveloped skill. Like conflict, confrontation produces anxiety and fear. Yet there is a way of engaging in confrontation that can be learned. It is a skill that develops gradually through a process of success and failure, perhaps with more failures than successes.

This may hold especially true for religiously-oriented people. A CARA study on alcoholism in religious communities discovered an interesting phenomenon.[1] People in the general population with a drinking problem are usually confronted a year before they themselves are aware of their problem. By contrast, members of religious communities are aware of their drinking problem a full year before any member of their community confronts them! Though the study was based on members of religious congregations, we presume that the findings are true for many other Catholic communities as well. Something endemic in the Christian culture makes it extremely difficult for Christians to confront one another, even though the confrontation is in the best interest of the person being confronted.

## Confrontation: What Is It?

Confrontation is a process that places the facts as they are perceived before another. It brings ideas and perceptions together for comparison and evaluation, and invites self-examination. It is an encounter that demands risk and pain, but the results can be most gratifying. Confrontation has the potential to "clear the air," reduce a generalized anxiety, and, in time, improve and deepen relationships with others.

Confrontation could be described as loving a person enough to give him or her information that is for the good of the person. It is the direct expression of one's perceptions of the behavior of another, combined with a loving invitation to the other to share his or her perceptions of the same behavior. It leads to clarifying and exploring the perceptions and the issues involved. Inherent in this encounter is the hope that the person will be able to hear the concern and possesses the resources to utilize the information which is shared.

Although difficult and threatening, confrontation is absolutely essential for the good of the individual and the community. Failure to confront can be harmful both for the individuals concerned and the community. An example of a community that neglected to confront will help to show the disastrous results when confrontation is avoided.

## When an Opportunity Is Missed

At a recent meeting, one of the community members, in what was his characteristic style, offered long, rambling, irrelevant comments on every issue on the agenda. Not surprisingly, the frustration and anger of the other members became evident in their countenance and body language: eyes rolled and knowing glances were shared. However, no one ever interrupted the speaker or commented on his inappropriate and counterproductive behavior. As often happens in "good communities," the comments that could have been presented at the meeting more appropriately and constructively were spoken in the safety and relative anonymity of small clusters in the parking lot. There, the frustration was vented but was never heard by the offending member. No constructive change resulted. Over time, the man's behavior continued and the members' frustration increased. Soon, members began to withdraw from the community, and the community, which had once had the potential to be a source of life for many, ceased to function.

Had an anonymous evaluation of that community's behavior been conducted, probably the frustration and anger toward the offending member would have been revealed. Unfortunately, this community is similar to other communities that allow themselves to be held captive by the tyranny of an individual. The passive, immature, and irresponsible behavior of the community members in this example provokes some questions. Why does a community passively endure frustrating and dysfunctional behavior? Why are the words spoken in the security of small cliques not voiced where they could assist the person and the community? Why are controlling members never confronted in a caring way that might help them see their behavior as the community experiences it? And finally, which is a greater detriment to the growth of the community: the controlling behavior of a single individual or the passivity of the community?

# Dysfunctional Passivity

In the above scenario, it is relatively easy to condemn the behavior of the dysfunctional member, but what often goes unchallenged is the dysfunctional behavior of the community: the unwillingness to confront. By its passivity, the community enables and reinforces the dysfunctional behavior of the member. One member cannot control the community unless the other members relinquish their authority by acting in a passive, immature way.

David McClelland, an outstanding researcher, was part of the FORUS study mentioned earlier. He studied members of communities who were identified by their leaders as "caring people." McClelland discovered that these caring individuals scored above the ninety-first percentile on a scale called "niceness." This percentile score gives cause for concern. These "nice" people would probably be extremely reluctant to deal with anger, hostility, conflict, and confrontation—all issues necessary for the growth of community. Failure to brave these issues signals the death knell of a community.

As described in chapter 1 and chapter 14, behavior is need-directed. In order to understand one's behavior or the behavior of others, it is important to identify the needs which produce that behavior. What needs in the previous example impeded the community from confronting the offending member? In a community, does the tyranny of an individual continue unchallenged because:

- to challenge it might threaten the comfort zone of individuals or a community (the need for safety and security)?
- we fear rejection (the need to belong)?
- we might not be liked (a psycho-social need)?
- we might not feel good about ourselves (the need for self-esteem)?

There is a more pernicious explanation of why a group fails to confront. By allowing or silently condoning the inappropriate behavior, the group is subtly scapegoating the individual. As long as the behavior continues, the community continues to expend its energy in condemning the perceived offending person and behavior. Channeling its energy in this fashion shields the community from the more difficult process of self-assessment. By focusing on the problematic member, the community is protected from having to face its own dysfunctional or inappropriate behavior. This is the essence of scapegoating. The passivity of the members justifies the continuation of the scapegoating.

Other possible explanations for the continuation of passive behavior continuing are that the members have an unconscious desire to see the group end or that, by enabling the behavior, they can justify departure from the group.

When a community complains that one person is unduly controlling the community and yet fails to take responsibility for confronting that person, the appropriate procedure is for a leader to focus on the passivity of the group. The questions that arise are, "Why does the group, by its passivity and collusion of silence, condone the behavior that it finds destructive?" and, "Why does the community not care enough to confront?"

Directly addressing individuals whose behavior is destructive to the growth of community is difficult and threatening because it often results in angry reactions, hostility, and eventual open conflict. Nevertheless, to confront shows respect for the other, while to protest about the offending party behind his or her back is disrespectful. Behavioral change can occur, but only in a climate of directness and gentleness.

This is not to suggest that confrontation is an easy task. Confrontation is always difficult and fraught with anxiety and fear. However, the choice to overlook the dysfunctional and disruptive behavior is disrespectful to the individual and destructive to the community.

## The Art of Confrontation

Basic to the art of confrontation is the attitude of the confronter. A genuine concern and care for the welfare of the individual and of the community are key ingredients if the confrontation is to be effective. When the person being confronted senses concern, there may be less defensiveness and greater openness to what is spoken. When insincerity is conveyed, the result is anxiety, defensiveness, and hostility. Before confronting another, the question to ask is, "Do I sincerely care about the person?"

Confrontations are most effective when judgment is suspended. The confronters report reality as they perceive it, understanding that perception may be inaccurate or incomplete. The goal of Christian confrontation is dialogue. Truth emerges in the dialogue that occurs when the confronter is willing to also hear the reality as the person confronted perceives it. "In confrontation, what do I convey to the other? Do I communicate that I expect the other to change his or her behavior as a result of what I have said? Do I offer the facts as I perceive them, and do I show interest in hearing how the other sees the situation? Is my goal to change the other or to establish a climate for dialogue?"

Productive dialogue is more likely to occur when the members of the group agree that they share in the responsibility to raise those issues which they perceive as destructive to an individual or to the life and purpose of the community. These expectations of responsibility are negotiated during the group orientation stage as part of the specifics of the group "contract." Mature groups accept the reality that, in all probability, there will be need for some confrontation and that honest dialogue is inevitable during the life of the community. A mutual contract empowers the members with both the obligation and right to confront. It also legitimizes confrontation and helps to lessen any negative aspects of later confrontations. As a community, have you identified areas where you invest each other with mutual accountability?

166

# Guidelines for Confronting

Table 16.1 offers some general guidelines that can contribute to achieving a successful confrontation.

## Table 16.1
## General Guidelines for Confronting

1.  Confront only when you can communicate your sincere concern and care for the other.

2.  Do not confront when you are feeling intense anger and frustration.

3.  Confront only when you are willing and open to hearing how the other person perceives the situation.

4.  When confronting, use personal "I" statements rather than "you" statements. "You" statements can be perceived as accusatory and can evoke a defensive reaction.

5.  When possible, confront with facts and not with opinions, inferences, or information gleaned from others.

6.  Use confrontation sparingly, only when you believe it will benefit the other and/or the community.

7.  Phrase the confrontation as information offered rather than as a demand.

8.  Direct the confrontation at concrete, specific behaviors rather than at abstract and generalized behaviors.

9.  State the confrontation directly and succinctly.

10. Represent facts as facts, hypotheses as hypotheses, and feelings as feelings.

11. Choose to confront at a time that will allow adequate dialogue after the initial confrontation.

12. Attempt to listen without any preconceived opinions about the other person. Try to communicate that you have heard both his or her content and feeling.

13. Do not impugn motives to the behavior confronted.

# Recommendations

In addition to the guidelines, here are further recommendations to consider:

## Allow time to reflect on the goodness and giftedness of the person being confronted.

The images and perceptions that you bring into the situation will influence directly the attitude you convey to the other person. If you are unable to conjure up positive images and qualities of the other person, your negativity will be experienced more strongly than any words you proclaim.

## Speak as directly as possible.

Vague and indirect statements raise the level of anxiety in the person being confronted. Anxiety increases defensiveness. Ideally, directness should be combined with gentleness. The combination of these two elements helps to create a positive climate. If you have confronted indirectly in the past, reflect on what fears influenced such behavior. Once these fears are identified, you can exert greater control over your manner and approach.

## Confront the behavior and not the person.

The recommendation to confront the behavior and not the person is a truism. It is much more difficult than it sounds. A person who is confronted will usually interpret the confrontation as a personal attack regardless of your intent. Thus you are best advised to *try* to keep the focus on the behavior, especially when there is an indication that the person feels personally attacked.

## Avoid interpreting a person's behavior.

This is probably the most important issue in confronting. Keep all comments descriptive while not attributing causes to the behavior. As soon as someone describes behavior and then adds, "and the reason you do that is . . . ," the listener will surely react. More damaging than attributing causes to behavior is to engage in pseudo-analysis and to label the person, e.g., "You are passive-aggressive," or, "You behave that way because you grew up in a dysfunctional family."

## Confrontation should be kept to issues that are recent, if not immediate.

Virginia Satir, the family therapist, often referred to "gunny-sacking," which, figuratively speaking, is a process of storing issues in a sack carried over one's shoulder. These past issues are extracted from the sack and brought inappropriately into present discussions. It is difficult enough for the person who is confronted to deal with the present, without trying mentally to resurrect and reconstruct the details of long-forgotten incidents. When the confronter begins enumerating past grievances, everyone involved becomes distracted.

Confrontation is rarely easy, but the possibility of its effectiveness is increased when some of the practical issues noted above are observed. At times in everyone's life, one is on the receiving end of confrontation. Here are some suggestions and recommendations that can help in receiving and benefiting from confrontation.

### Table 16.2
## Attitudes of the Confrontee

1. Accept the confrontation as an invitation to explore oneself.

2. Attempt to remain open to hearing how others perceive you.

3. Realize that confrontation will result in personal disorganization and the need to reassess one's sense of identity.

4. Try to refrain from responding to confrontation in your stereotypical way of responding to any threat.

5. Listen to what is being said and ask for clarification where there is any ambiguity or unclarity. Reflect on what has been shared before responding.

## Individual or Group Confrontation

Whether confrontation is a communal or an individual issue is a common question. When the behavior is pathological or self-destructive, group or communal interventions are probably the most effective. However, this chapter has referred to disruptive rather than pathological behavior. Given this fact, it is probably more feasible for an individual to create a climate and atmosphere that will facilitate a person's acceptance of the confrontation. A communal confrontation increases the possibility of the person's feeling overwhelmed by the sheer number of confronters.

There is a distinction between confrontation and intervention. An intervention occurs when someone with authority attempts to arrest the self- or other-destructive behavior of another. Confrontation is a process initiated out of a genuine concern for the other. Its goal is dialogue. At times when confrontation is not effective and the person's behavior is of a serious nature, often requiring treatment, an intervention is warranted.

## Summary

Dysfunctional or tyrannical behavior often perdures in community because the members fear challenging and confronting such behavior. Challenge and confrontation are the mature and potentially constructive responses to such behavior. When dysfunctional behavior is allowed to continue and the community is unwilling to engage in a process of confrontation, then the members need to explore the reasons why they have allowed such disruptive and destructive behavior to continue. The passivity of the group is a greater threat to the growth of the community than the tyrannical behavior.

Confrontation is always difficult. It is a skill that takes time to develop, and the learner may experience apparent failures in the process. The potential for positive results is greater when such aspects as determining clear reasons for confronting, attending to practical aspects, and developing the skill of confrontation are kept in focus.

## Suggested Readings

Augsburger, David. *Caring Enough to Confront*. Ventura, CA: Regal Books, 1982, pp. 13-52.

Clark, Keith. *The Skilled Participant*. Notre Dame, IN: Ave Maria Press, 1988, pp. 49-62.

Hart, Richard, O.F.M. Cap., M.A., "The Gift of Confrontation," *Human Development*, Vol. 16, #3, Fall 1995.

Sofield, Loughlan and Carroll Juliano. *Collaborative Ministry: Skills and Guidelines*. Notre Dame, IN: Ave Maria Press, 1987, pp. 117-123.

## Reflection Questions

1. Can I identify behavior in our community that I believe is controlling and manipulative?
2. Can I identify the reasons why I, or we, do not confront this behavior?
3. Why am I unwilling to confront, even when it is in the best interest of an individual or the community? What fears stop me from confronting?
4. Can I identify positive experiences of confrontation that I have observed or been involved in? What were the elements that contributed toward these positive experiences?

# Process for Group Sharing

1. Discuss the fears that might prevent the members from being completely honest about confronting behavior which is perceived as being disruptive to the growth of the community.
2. Openly discuss the behavior that each member believes is not conducive to community growth.
3. Determine how the community proposes to deal with such behavior.
4. Discuss any positive experiences of confrontation identified by the members and the elements that contributed to those positive experiences.
5. Decide to spend fifteen to twenty minutes at the end of every third or fourth meeting, evaluating how faithful the members are to speaking the truth necessary for the good of the individual and the community.

# 17
# *Community in Scripture*

*I pray . . . they all be one, just as, Father,*
*you are in me and I am in you, so that*
*they also may be in us.*
*—John 17:20-21*

This prayer of Jesus which appears toward the conclusion of his last discourse reflects his ultimate wish for each of his followers: complete union with him and his heavenly Father. The depths of Jesus' desire for communion are evidenced by the fact that these sentiments are repeated a number of times in this discourse. What stronger love could Jesus express than his wish that we, the people of God, share the same communion that he shares with his Father?

The prayer of John 17 is the summit of the theme of union with God that courses throughout sacred scripture. In Genesis, God decreed that we should be made "in our own image, in the likeness of ourselves . . ." (Gn 1:26). The human race is, therefore, a reflection of God. And God is community: three persons, one God. To the degree that the followers of Jesus become more communal, they become visible signs of God's abiding presence in the world.

Scripture is the ever-unfolding story of the development of a people. Within these sacred passages exists innumerable lessons for all Christian communities. What follows is not a scholarly exegesis of the scriptures. Instead, we have chosen to focus on a few key issues that can provide insights into the development of community. The issues we have chosen from the Old Testament are: God's covenant with community, the attraction-and-avoidance cycle evidenced by the Old Testament community, and the differing roles of the leadership figures of this covenant community. From the New Testament we have limited our observations to some qualities that characterized those early church communities. In light of the Old and New Testament, we project the reader into the present, to the "Now Community."

173

## The Call to Community in the Old Testament

The Bible is the story of God's action in history. Throughout the ages God has repeatedly chosen a people—a community—as the means for carrying out his mission. Leviticus speaks of God's promise to dwell in and with this community forever: "I shall fix my home among you and never reject you. I shall live among you; I shall be your God and you will be my people" (26:11-12). This promise of God's abiding presence is a continuation of a covenant described in Genesis 28:10-22. These passages describe Jacob's dream in which God promises to give the land, not to Jacob alone, but to his descendants throughout all of history.

The Old Testament is replete with examples of the community's commitment to be faithful to Yahweh, followed by long periods of unfaithfulness and rejection. Yahweh was never unfaithful, and whenever the Israelites acknowledged their unfaithfulness, God received them back with a loving embrace.

From among all the nations of the world, God selected this chosen community to be a sign of salvation. In Exodus, Yahweh directly informs them of their unique call, "you, out of all peoples, shall be my personal possession . . ." (19:5-6).

This chosen community encompassed all the best and worst elements of community. Careful reading of the sacred texts, which chronicle the history of these people, reveals a cycle that repeated itself continually throughout their life.

### Table 17.1
## The Cycle of Community Found in the Old Testament

1. The community experiences a call from the Lord.
2. The initial response to this call is characterized by love and faithfulness.
3. After a period of relative faithfulness, there is a strong attraction away from God.
4. This attraction often leads to a rupture and alienation, in the relationship between God and his people, to sinfulness.
5. The all-loving God, refusing to remain passive, repeatedly reaches out to the community to restore the relationship and the unity.
6. Throughout history the responses of the Chosen People vary. Some accept the invitation to re-establish the loving oneness and others do not.
7. The cycle is repeated in an ever-evolving dance of attraction, rejection, alienation, and loving response.

The Old Testament community was a covenant community. God covenanted with Abraham, Isaac, Jacob, and Moses. This bound them to each other and to God. In Exodus 19:5-6 we read, "if you will obey my voice and keep my covenant, you shall be my own possession among all peoples . . . and you shall be to me a kingdom of priests and a holy nation." God promised to remain faithful even if they were unfaithful (Hos 10:11-12 and Is 1:24-28).

God's covenant was never just with an individual; it was a covenant with the people, with the community (Is 5:26-29 and 1 Kgs 20:8-15). God continued to communicate with this community and to solidify this covenant through the mouths of the prophets. God never abandoned his people but continued to manifest the divine Self through words and deeds as the one, true, and living God. Through these manifestations Israel gained a deeper and clearer understanding of God's ways.

## Leadership in the Old Testament

This covenant community saw a procession of leaders. Each offered a different gift and a different role that responded to the changing needs of the community.

Abraham held a preeminent role among this community. His call was to be the father of a new people, "I shall make you a great nation . . . and all clans on earth will bless themselves by you" (Gn 12:2-3). Referred to as our "father in faith," Abraham's role was that of parent-leader.

Moses' destiny was leading a group of slaves from Egypt into freedom and community in order to become a new people of God. Moses' role was to be a liberating leader. However, like many communal leaders, he was reluctant, "Who am I to go to Pharaoh and bring the Israelites out of Egypt?" (Ex 3:11).

Joshua brought the people together and proclaimed an invitation to share in God's life. Joshua gathered the Israelites together at the end of his life and exhorted them to be faithful to the Lord: "You must make up your minds whom you do wish to serve. . . . As regards my family and me, we shall serve Yahweh" (Jos 24:15). Joshua was the gathering leader.

Isaiah (2:1-4) foretold the transforming role of Israel. He declared that Israel would eventually shine forth as a sign among nations. After they had experienced transformation, Israel would become the mediator through whom God would be revealed to the other nations. Isaiah was the transforming leader.

### Table 17.2
# Four Models of Old Testament Leadership

| PERSON | MODEL |
|--------|-------|
| Abraham | Parent-Leader |
| Moses | Liberating Leader |
| Joshua | Gathering Leader |
| Isaiah | Transforming Leader |

This seemingly random selection of leaders was truly divinely inspired and presages all future communities. No single type of individual can be the perennial effective leader. Different periods in the growth of community call for different forms of leadership. During the initial phase, all communities need parental, mother-father leaders, who give gentle, loving birth to the community. After the departure of this founding leader, the community, at times, stagnates in a maudlin nostalgia for the past. At this point it requires a liberating leader who will free the community from the restraints of the past and move them to embrace the present and to create the future.

At different points in the life of community, other forms of leadership are required. Sometimes there is need for a gathering leader who helps the community to be faithful to the essence of who they have been called to be as community. At other times they require a transforming leader who will lead them from their safety, security, and comfort into an apostolic, generative community.

Different moments in the life of a community demand different styles and gifts of leadership. Reflect on your present community and ask, "Based on where we are as a community, what type of leadership do we now need?"

# The Call to Community in the New Testament

In the fullness of time, God spoke through Jesus Christ, the Word made Flesh. The Old Testament community was a precursor of the New Testament community that was formed in the presence of Jesus.

This community, gathered by Jesus and described in the New Testament, was characterized by many distinguishing elements. We have selected only three characteristics as possible criteria against which to examine our present communities.

- Jesus' community was one of love, forgiveness, and healing.
- It was a transforming community.
- It was a community that had an apostolic mission.

### A Loving, Forgiving, Healing Community

Pope John Paul II in *Redemptoris Missio* (chapter 2) declares, "The Kingdom aims at transforming relationships; it grows gradually as people slowly learn to love, forgive and serve one another." These three qualities of loving, forgiving, and serving (or healing) are the qualities that distinguished the life of Jesus and his initial community members. In his letter to the Ephesians, Saint Paul, after challenging the members to rid themselves of all the attitudes and behaviors that destroy community, invites them to assume these three characteristics, "be kind to one another, compassionate, and mutually forgiving" (4:32).

Jesus's community was marked by love. Like the divine Master, this community was distinguished by its loving compassion. Jesus constantly looked upon people with the heart of compassion (Mt 9:36). When asked by the Pharisees which is the greatest commandment, Jesus responded instantly, "You must love the Lord your God with all your heart. . . . You must love your neighbor as yourself" (Mt 22:37-39). In case the community failed to grasp the centrality of this message, Jesus models it in the washing of the feet (Jn 13) and states it unambiguously in the last discourse, "I give you a new commandment: love one another" (Jn 13:34). Jesus left no doubt that this call to love was a call to an ever expanding love. He challenged his disciples not only to love their neighbors (Mt 19:19) but also their enemies (Mt 5:44).

The early followers of Jesus tried to make this quality of love and compassion the hallmark of their communal life. They shared their lives together as well as their possessions (Acts 4:32). All, regardless of social status, were invited to partake of their friendship and experienced the "living waters" of the compassionate Christlike community.

In the document quoted earlier, *Redemptoris Missio*, Pope John Paul II declares, "Two gestures are characteristic of Jesus' mission: healing and forgiving." A dominant message of Jesus is forgiveness of others. He makes it a condition for being forgiven and includes it in the prayer to his heavenly Father, "Yes, if you forgive others their failings, your heavenly Father will forgive you yours; but if you do not forgive others, your Father will not forgive your failings either (Mt 6:14-15). One of the final acts of Jesus was modeling complete selfless forgiveness: "Father, forgive them; they do not know what they are doing" (Lk 23:34).

The four evangelists recorded numerous cures and healings performed by Jesus. Saint Matthew says that he, "cured all who were sick" (8:16). The healing of the afflicted did not end with the death of Jesus but was continued by the early apostolic community. In the Acts of the Apostles there are numerous examples of physical and spiritual healing: the man who was "a cripple from birth" (3:2); "the sick and those tormented by unclean spirits" (5:16); "the possessed . . . paralytics and cripples" (8:7).

## A Transforming Community

Throughout the gospel it is evident that Christ was overwhelmingly aware of human weaknesses. Yet, he looked beyond mere human limitations and saw the potential of every individual. Aware of this potential, Jesus worked to transform the person. These interactions with Jesus always resulted in healing and in physical, emotional, and spiritual growth. Touched by the Lord, those individuals were transformed to be stronger and more faithful (Lk 13:11-13; Jn 4:28-29, 39). He called individuals to be transformed, "to repent" (Mt 3:2) and be changed.

Jesus not only transformed individuals, but he strove to reconstruct long-held values that were not consonant with those of the kingdom. The Beatitudes (Mt 5:1-12) epitomize this. Jesus endeavored to effect this transformation, not only by his preaching, but also by his actions. He ate with sinners (Mt 9-13), he spoke directly to the Samaritan woman (Jn 4).

Jesus' witness converted the members of his community. Then, this community, through their experience of being of one mind and heart with him, sought to bring God's loving presence into every corner of their world.

Jesus promised the abiding presence of the Holy Spirit to the succeeding generations of Christian communities. The Holy Spirit continues the process of transforming Christian communities into communities of love (Jn 16:19-26 and 17:1-26).

### An Apostolic Community—A Community of Disciples

The community that Jesus formed did not spend exorbitant amounts of time and energy creating community. They were an apostolic community, a community in mission, "a community of disciples" to quote Avery Dulles.[1] Jesus not only gathered the community, he scattered it. He called disciples to come rest with him and then sent them out in mission. Saint Matthew divulges the historic mission of the twelve disciples . . . being sent by Jesus to proclaim the Messiah, the reign of God, to the "lost sheep of Israel" (10:1-6).

Their apostolic endeavors were many. They strove to gather Israel back to God and to reform a covenant community. Through and with Jesus they sought to draw together an Israel fractured by struggling parties and groups. The needs to which this apostolic community responded were many. Jesus declares, "The harvest is rich but the laborers are few, so ask the Lord of the harvest to send out laborers to his harvest" (Mt. 9:37).

When Israel as a whole did not respond, the circle of disciples acquired a new function. It received the task of representing symbolically what should have taken place in Israel as a whole: complete dedication to the gospel of the reign of God, a radical conversion to a new way of life, and a gathering of brothers and sisters into community (Lk 8:1). Jesus' community of the Twelve is symbolic of the whole of Israel—a symbol of what Israel was intended to become, an evangelizing community of disciples (Rev 7:4-12, Jn 13:16-17 and 17:17).

# The Now Community

The community of Jesus did not cease with the death of Jesus or the culmination of the apostolic period. After Jesus' death and resurrection the word of God continued to be spread throughout the world, first by the apostles and then by Christian witnesses and missionaries of every age. Now the word of God is entrusted to all of us today. By baptism we are called to be the new community, the "Now Community." Christ said: "If you make my word your home you will indeed be my disciples" (Jn 8:31). "It is by your love for one another, that everyone will recognize you as my disciples" (Jn 13:35). Through insertion by baptism into the Christian community, all are called to be the "living community" (Eph 1:22-23) participating in the prophetic mission of Jesus to witness God's love for all creation (Lk 24:36-43, Jn 20:26-29, Rom 1:1-5, 1 Cor 1:17).

The pentecost event was the explicit transition from the New Testament community to the "Now Community." The outpouring of the Spirit at Pentecost was not to isolated persons, but rather a gift to the gathered and scattered community. The Spirit was given to the Body of Christ—the community throughout all ages (1 Cor 6:19-20, Jn 6:56, Eph 2:19-22).

God's call to participate in community, to live in his image and likeness, was not restricted to the Israelites or the early apostolic community. It is a perennial, eternal call. In responding to this call, confirmed in baptism, each person discovers the fullness of his or her divine call to discipleship.

God's call to community is a living message spoken today just as truly as it was to Abraham, Isaac, Jacob, and Moses, i.e., to the people of Israel. The invitation is as real as was the call to James, John, Matthew, Peter, Mary, Martha, and all the early disciples.

Community is not a question of choice. To be human is to live in community, in relationship. Divine intimacy is the final goal of one's total being. "Our hearts are restless till they rest in you," as St. Augustine said. The questions for us are: How well will I live in community? How visible in my life is the example of Christ? Can we be the visible sign of God's action in the world today through our own witness to community?

As many grains of wheat become one bread, so the Christian community is always in the process of becoming one, a witness to God's call to unity. Of its very nature it is missionary: it has a mission of service to the gospel, to be a sign of witness to the Kingdom of God where there is neither Greek nor Gentile, neither slave nor free, neither male nor female—to be a sign of love.

## Summary

God selected out of many peoples of the world a single people to make them a visible sign of salvation.

Jesus personally appropriated this prophetic interpretation of God's history with the world, this understanding of Israel's history of election. For, even after Israel as a whole refused his message, Jesus did not abandon the idea of community, the idea that the reign of God must have a people. Instead he concentrated on his circle of disciples. He bound the reign of God to his community of disciples. As Luke puts it: "There is no need to be afraid, little flock, for it has pleased your Father to give you the kingdom" (12:32).

> God's covenant is universal and extends beyond the Old Testament times into our present age. God's call to community is a living message spoken today—just as truly as it was to Abraham, Isaac, Jacob, and Moses, i.e., to the people of Israel.

## Suggested Readings

Gish, Arthur. *Living in Christian Community*. Scottdale, PA: Herald Press, 1979.

Keating, Charles. *Community*. St. Meinrad, IN: Abbey Press, 1977, chapter 1.

Lohfink, Gerhard. *Jesus and Community*. New York: Paulist Press.

Westley, Dick. *Redemptive Intimacy*. Mystic, CT: Twenty-Third Publications, 1982.

## Reflection Questions

1. In what ways do we see ourselves as a covenant community?
2. What type of leadership is needed to foster the growth of our community at this time?
3. What do you believe are the major characteristics of the New Testament community? In what way are we challenged by those characteristics?
4. What does it mean to be the "Now Community"?

## Process for Group Sharing
### Process 1

1. Select a scripture passage that speaks of community. Some suggested readings are: Acts 2:42-47, Acts 4:32-37, John 17:17-21, 1 Corinthians 11:17-34, Romans 12, 1 Corinthians 12.
2. After listening to the proclaiming of the word of God, ask yourself the following questions:
   a) What is God saying to me through this passage?
   b) What is God saying to us as a community?
3. Invite each member to share his or her reflections on these two questions.
4. Listen to each sharing without any response.
5. Encourage open discussion to attempt to discern where the Spirit is leading you through this reflection and discussion.

## Process 2

1. Ask each member to select his or her favorite Old Testament and New Testament passages that speak of community.
2. Invite them to describe what aspects of the Old Testament community or New Testament community speak to them regarding this community.
3. Try to identify what characteristics of the Old and New Testament you hope would describe you as a community.
4. Discuss what specifically would have to occur in this community for us to more effectively reflect these characteristics.

# Epilogue:
# Building Our Community

This book has provided material related to issues which we, the authors, have identified as integral for building community. However, each community is unique and has different issues that it must address. Therefore, we invite the members of the community to develop additional chapters that are especially relevant for your group.

The process is as follows:

1. Identify additional issues that are not included in this book but are important for your community.
2. Develop a few pages describing the issue.
3. Recommend a few readings related to the topic.
4. Offer some questions for personal reflection.
5. Propose a process for utilizing this material at a future meeting.

# Notes

## Introduction

1. National Conference of Catholic Bishops. *Sons and Daughters of the Light: A Pastoral Plan for Ministry with Young Adults*. Washington, DC: United States Catholic Conference, 1997, p. 19ff.
2. Roof, Wade Clark. *A Generation of Seekers: The Spiritual Journeys of the Baby Boom Generation*. HarperCollins, 1993.
3. Gallup, George and Jim Castelli. *The People's Religion: American Faith in the 90's*. New York: Macmillan Publishing Company, 1989.
4. Brennan, Frank, "The Bill of Rights and the Supreme Court: A Foreigner's View," *America*, Vol. 174, No. 12, April 13, 1996.
5. Brophy, Don, "Why I Don't Pray Anymore," *National Catholic Reporter*, March 1, 1971.

## Chapter 1

1. Hammett, Rosine and Loughlan Sofield. *Inside Christian Community*. New York: Jesuit Educational Center for Human Development (Le Jacq Publishing), 1981.
2. Erikson, Erik. *Childhood and Society*. New York: W.W. Norton and Co., 1963.
3. Leege, David, "Parish Life Among the Leaders," *Notre Dame Study of Catholic Parish Life*, University of Notre Dame, Report #9, December 1986.

## Chapter 2

1. Friedman, Edwin H., "Emotional Process in the Marketplace: The Family Therapist as Consultant with Work Systems" in McDaniel, Susan, Lyman Wynn, and Timothy Weber. *Systems Consultation: A New Perspective for Families*. New York: Guilford, 1986.

## Chapter 4

1. Erikson, Erik, *Childhood and Society*. New York: W.W. Norton and Co., 1963.

## Chapter 5

1. National Conference of Catholic Bishops. *Called and Gifted: The American Catholic Laity*. Washington, DC: USCC, 1980; and *Called and Gifted for the Third Millennium*. Washington, DC: USCC, 1995.
2. McAllister, Robert J. *Living the Vows: The Emotional Conflicts of Celibate Religious*. San Francisco: Harper and Row, 1986.
3. Meissner, William W. *Group Dynamics in the Religious Life*. Notre Dame, IN: University of Notre Dame Press, 1965.
4. Nygren, David and Miriam Ukeritis, "Research Executive Summary: Future of Religious Orders in the United States," *Origins*, September 24, 1992, Vol. 22: No. 15.
5. Sacred Congregation for Religious and Secular Institutes. *Essential Elements in the Church's Teaching on Religious Life as Applied to Institutes Dedicated to Works of the Apostolate*. Issued by the Vatican, May 31, 1983.

## Chapter 6

1. *Biography*, Interview with Angela Lansbury by Barbara Walters, Arts and Entertainment Network.
2. Burkert, William and Loughlan Sofield, "Unwrapping Your Gifts," *Human Development*, Vol. 7, #2, Summer 1996, pp. 43-46.
3. National Conference of Catholic Bishops. *Called and Gifted for the Third Millennium: Reflections of the U.S. Catholic Bishops on the Thirtieth Anniversary of the Decree on the Apostolate of the Laity and the Fifteenth Anniversary of Called and Gifted*. Washington, DC: NCCB/USCC, 1995.
4. "Decree on the Apostolate of the Laity," *Documents of the Second Vatican Council*, #3.

## Chapter 7

1. Kelly, Brian J., "Family Theory Lends Support to Spirituality," *Human Development*, Vol. 17, #2, Summer 1996, pp. 43-47.
2. Ibid.

3. Carmody, Denise. *Christian Feminist Theology: A Constructive Interpretation*. Cambridge, MA: Blackwell, 1995.

## Chapter 8

1. Pope John Paul II. *On the Permanent Validity of the Church's Missionary Mandate*. An Encyclical Letter. December 7, 1990.
2. Smedes, Lewis B. *Forgive and Forget*. San Francisco: Harper and Row, 1984.
3. ABC Transcript #1701, January 3, 1997.
4. Enright, Robert and Alii. *Interpersonal Forgiveness Within the Helping Professions: An Attempt to Resolve Differences of Opinions*. University of Wisconsin-Madison, September 1991.
5. Quoted in David Gill, "Making Sense of Martyrdom," *Human Development*, Fall 1991, Vol. 12, #3, pp. 44-47.

## Chapter 9

1. Catholic Bishops Conference of England, Wales, and Scotland. *Briefing*, November 16, 1995.
2. Dulles, Avery. *A Church to Believe In*. New York: Crossroads Books: Seabury Press, 1982.
3. *New Evangelization, Human Development, Christian Culture*, Fourth General Conference of Latin American Bishops, Santo Domingo, Dominican Republic, Oct.12-18, 1992, #55.
4. Ibid., #61
5. Cowan, Michael and Bernard Lee. *The Future Content of Dangerous Memories: The Inner and Public Life of Small Christian Communities*. Orbis, 1997.
6. Dulles, Avery, "John Paul II and the New Evangelization," *America*, February 1, 1992, Vol. 166, #3, pp. 52-72.
7. National Conference of Catholic Bishops. *Sons and Daughters of the Light: A Pastoral Plan for Ministry with Young Adults*. Washington, DC: USCC, 1996.

## Chapter 10

1. Russell, Letty. *The Future of Partnership*. Philadelphia: Westminster Press, 1979.

## Chapter 12

1. Erikson, Erik. *Childhood and Society*. New York: W.W. Norton and Co., 1963.

## Chapter 14

1. Morgan, Thomas, "The Heart of Ministry," *Human Development*, Vol. 15, #4, Winter 1995 (mistakenly labeled 1994), pp. 34-36.

## Chapter 16

1. Center for Applied Research in the Apostolate. *Culture of Recovery, Culture of Denial: Alcoholism Among Men and Women Religious*. (Eleace King, IHM and Jim Castelli). Washington, DC: Georgetown University, 1995.

## Chapter 17

1. Dulles, Avery. *A Church to Believe In*. New York: Crossroads Books: Seabury Press, 1982.

# Authors

**Br. Loughlan Sofield, S.T.**, a leading consultant on ministry and personal development, lectures and gives workshops across the United States as well as internationally. In 1990 he collaborated with Rosine Hammett and Carroll Juliano on *Design for Wholeness: Dealing with Anger, Learning to Forgive, Building Self-Esteem*, and in 1987 with Carroll Juliano on *Collaborative Ministry: Skills and Guidelines* (both published by Ave Maria Press). In 1996 his book with Donald Kuhn, *The Collaborative Leader*, was awarded first place by the Catholic Press Association for the field of pastoral ministry. He is senior editor of *Human Development* magazine and a member of the Missionary Servants of the Most Holy Trinity.

**Sr. Rosine Hammett, C.S.C., Ph.D.**, is a member of the Congregation of the Sisters of the Holy Cross at Notre Dame, Indiana. As a therapist, lecturer, communications consultant, and facilitator of personal growth groups, she has worked in North and South America, Asia, Israel, and Africa. She also directs retreats and gives spiritual direction. She coauthored *Inside Christian Community* and *Design for Wholeness* and has published articles in *Human Development* and *Sisters Today*.

**Sr. Carroll Juliano, S.H.C.J.**, a member of the Society of the Holy Child Jesus, is currently serving on the congregation's leadership team of the American Province. Her background in education includes teaching, administration, and counseling. She has offered presentations throughout the United States, Canada, Asia, Europe, Africa, and Australia. Carroll has authored numerous articles and books. She is coauthor of *Collaborative Ministry: Skills and Guidelines* and *Design for Wholeness: Dealing With Anger, Learning to Forgive and Building Self-Esteem*.